Ouch! that hurts

by
Arwyn Bailey

Galactic Publishers Limited.

Roxeth House
Shaftesbury Avenue
Harrow
Middlesex
HA2 0PZ

w: http://www.galacticpublishers.net/

First published in Great Britain in 2010.

Text Copyright © Arwyn Bailey 2010.

Galactic Publishers Limited does not necessarily endorse the individual views contained in its publications.

The author and the publisher have made every effort to ensure that any external websites and emails referenced in this work are up to date and in existence. Neither the publisher not the author is responsible for the continuing access to any site or email address referred to, nor are they responsible for the content of any such source.

All rights reserved. No part of this book may be reproduced, stored in, or introduced to any form of retrieval system, or transmitted in any form or by any means (electronic or mechanical, including photocopying, recording or otherwise) without the prior permission being gained in writing from the publisher. Any person who does any unauthorised act in relation to this publication may be liable to criminal prosecution and civil claims for damages. This book is sold subject to the condition that it shall not be lent, re-sold, hired out, or otherwise circulated in any form of binding or cover other than that in which it is published and without a similar condition including this condition being imposed on the subsequent purchaser.

Scripture quotations taken from the HOLY BIBLE, NEW INTERNATIONAL VERSION. Copyright © 1973, 1978, 1984 by International Bible Society. Used by permission of Hodder & Stoughton Publishers, a member of the Hachette UK Group. All rights reserved. "NIV" is a registered trademark of International Bible Society. UK trademark number 1448790.

A catalogue record for this book is available from the British Library.

ISBN 978-1-907665-23-3

Typeset by Galactic Publishers Limited, Harrow, Middlesex.
Printed and bound in England by Inform Print North Harrow, Middlesex.

*This book is dedicated to my amazing wife, Helen.
I would be lost without you.*

Contents

Preface	—	vii
Are You Sitting Uncomfortably	—	11
He Started It	—	37
A Sound Business Proposition	—	55
Neither a Borrower Nor a Lender Be	—	67
Lend us a Tenner Mate	—	83
Possession is Nine Tenths of the Law	—	105
Cash is King	—	123
How Much!	—	145
Greedy Bleeping Bleepers	—	161
The Fight Back	—	185
Here Endeth Today's Lesson	—	197
Author's Note	—	213
Action Points	—	215
Useful Sites and Contacts	—	217
Suggested Reading	—	219

PREFACE

Before sitting down and writing a book there must be a motive for doing so. Within this process an author should consider, and pose the hard question, should the book be written at all?

Bearing all of this in mind, I decided to persevere and write this book. One reason for this decision is that I have become disillusioned with the manner of reporting that has been deployed during the so called: "Credit Crunch". Some missives have been very emotional, some—I am sure—have contained a certain amount of political bias. I firmly believe that it has become necessary to redress this balance somewhat and look at what has caused the credit crunch and the subsequent drama of the banking crisis.

I hope that I have managed to express a viewpoint that is founded upon my faith, that stems from the scriptures that we have all come to label as the Holy Bible, and this collection of ancient writings talks about wealth, a great deal, as we will discover. Little mainstream public comment has been made, upon this economic crisis, by faith groups and those that could be labelled as the "prophets" of today.

I also wrote this book partly out of self interest. I wanted to discover for myself, as an Independent Financial Adviser, what I should think of all that has occurred. Can I find any answers within my own faith? What foundations are there within scripture that I can hold on to during this crisis? I must confess, beyond that of trying to act honestly, I did not really know how to relate Biblical teaching on wealth, to that of the city based investments that I advise upon on a daily basis.

The over-riding reason for writing this tome is, however, a simple one. I have come to realise that we cannot blame a solitary sector of society for the largest crash in the world's economies that mankind has ever seen. And, if we wish to apportion blame, I wanted to discover who should bear the brunt of our ire?

In examining this crisis I have looked at wealth in general, the wider implications of handling wealth in the many different aspects of our lives from charitable giving, to Bankers' bonuses, irresponsible lending policies etc…

So they are the reasons, now some brief pointers for you. When referring to the historical figure that we call Jesus, I have used his Hebrew name of Yeshua with the anglicised name—Jesus—in brackets alongside. Please use whatever form for his name that you feel comfortable with as you read the text.

When referring to Bankers, I have taken the liberty of giving them the title, Banker or Bankers, therefore these words are normally capitalised.

Now to the necessary gratitude. (Please note that all of these wonderful people may not agree with all that I have written and their inclusion does not constitute an endorsement. That is the beauty of free thought and debate.)

Thank you to my friend Bruce Collins for reading the initial manuscript and for offering so many helpful suggestions to me. Without your wisdom and insight, this book would never have seen the light of day.

I must also thank Trevor Rodgers. You are one of the unsung heroes who helped so courageously in the aftermath of the atrocious 7/7 bombings. After reading my first book, Noah & the Giraffe—due to your kind comments—you have encouraged me to continue writing and this is the end result. For this I thank you.

To my friend of many years, John Price, entrepreneur, accountant, business brain, and now a local debt counsellor. For your compassion and enthusiasm that is unbounded, for your kind comments, encouragement and contributions to this book, I thank you. (I also make this long overdue public apology. I am sorry for asking you be the ass, in my re-telling of the story of Esther all those years ago. It did prove that your back was strong, very strong indeed.)

I must thank my mentor, Peter Took, who helped me and advised me so much, when I entered into the world of financial services. You offered me so much advice when I took those first tentative steps into this amazing world. Like a toddler on their first day at school, you took me by the hand and led me through the maze of employment opportunities. Enjoy your retirement, you deserve it.

To Keith Tondeur. You are a tireless campaigner on behalf of the desolate and broken. You bring hope to hopeless situations and you are changing society step by step, and you are bringing the love of Christ into people's lives. Thank you for reading the draft manuscript and for your willingness to offer a comment.

To all those at CAP, in particular Josie, thank you for being willing to permit me to use the name of your organisation in this book. All of you who work at CAP, with your nation of debt counsellors, are a beacon of hope. Your aim to bring relief from debt to so many, is a hope for this nation.

To Patrick Wilford. You are simply amazing. Your work in Maseno has opened the eyes of many and has bought independence and hope to many of the poorest of the poor. Thank you for letting me tag along with you on trip after trip to Kenya. You have taught me so much about faith and compassion for the poor and dispossessed.

To Derek and John, my anonymous "Bankers". Thank you for being willing to give your time freely in an interview. You opened the door when others declined me the opportunity. Your contribution is invaluable. I hope that I have done you justice. You both carry the torch of hope, honesty and integrity in the largest financial market in the world through the advice that you give.

To Danny, my son-in-law. Thank you for your analytical comments upon my first book. Your theological insight is so necessary and important in this world, at this time. I hope that you enjoy this book as much as you have enjoyed my earlier work. I look forward to your critique of my theology within this book.

Thank you to the many other named and unnamed people in this little book. I hope that you understand that I have tried to be fair in relating your stories, hopes, aspirations and dreams. Any errors or misrepresentation is not intentional, I assure you.

Finally, to my long suffering wife. For tolerating me day after day and for your endurance—during many evenings—of my tapping away at my computer keyboard; and for your sacrifice and understanding, I thank you. I love you more each day. The past twenty five years have been a blast. Like a vintage wine, our marriage will "improve" yet further, with age. Thank you so much for everything.

Arwyn Bailey.

CHAPTER ONE

ARE YOU SITTING UNCOMFORTABLY?

If you were to make a list of who you consider to be wealthy, I wonder who would make it onto your own rich list? Would any of the following: Bill Gates, Richard Branson, Donald Trump, Alan Sugar, the Sultan of Brunei? Or would it be someone else entirely? How about sports stars such as: David Beckham, Michael Jordan, Lewis Hamilton etc…? What about those in showbiz, like: Simon Cowell, Cheryl Cole, Jennifer Lopez, Tom Cruise, Madonna? You might name some other idol, or celebrity. Your list could be very long and—depending upon when you read this—your choice might be influenced by who is in vogue at the time.

But what about you? Have you ever considered whether you are rich? And if so, just how rich are you?

Before you read any further, I must warn in advance that I write as a Christian and I believe that the Holy Bible has a lot to say about the subject of wealth. As the scriptures of my faith has so much to say, it must be assumed that money and wealth is of concern to this named God of the Holy Bible. This means that I will delve and dig about in the scriptures in order to gain clarity, before drawing any firm conclusions.

I also believe that many of the principles outlined in the pages of the Holy Bible can be used by all, no matter what belief one might hold, so please do not discard this book even if you have no (or little) faith. I also believe that the Holy Bible is my arbitrator, judge and jury. I believe that it is within the pages of scriptures that ultimate truth can be discovered as it is a unique book. The book does not start at the beginning—God was in existence prior to the beginning—neither does it end at the end—it boasts of a glory beyond the termination of the current earth. I believe that these truths transcend history, race and culture and that they are as valid for us today—and the fast paced society in which we live—as they were when they were first written.

I would like to stress that it is not my intention to make anyone feel guilty in what I write, but wealth is something that can influence us quite markedly. It can colour our perception of one another quite significantly.

If you are sitting comfortably then we will begin to examine this whole arena of wealth, the credit crunch, and the banking crisis by firstly pondering upon our own corporate attitude to wealth. Let's kick off with a quote about making a fortune. The American oil magnate J.P. Getty is often cited as a man of a considerable riches. He is quoted often. Perhaps his most famous mantra relates to his own formula for the successful acquisition of wealth. He stated that to become rich you need to:

> Rise early, work hard, and strike oil.

What do you think of this statement? My immediate thought is to wonder if this is a realistic and achievable goal for me, or for you, even if either of us wished to acquire a fortune beyond our wildest dreams? It is safe to assume that we are highly unlikely to strike oil; and even if we were fortunate enough to do so then our strike may be out of date very shortly, as renewable energy may overtake our society's need for crude oil. We may find that we are holding onto a worthless asset. So, if we want to become a millionaire, what options are left open to enable us to walk down the corridor of fame and fortune? Is there a decent honest short-cut? (Gain wealth quickly was not only the Bankers' mantra, as we will see.)

No matter where you might stand on the issue of wealth, I can almost guarantee that you desire the best (however this might be defined) for: yourself; your children; and those that you love. You may want a good standard of living and to be successful (however this might be defined). You might like to have good holidays; live in a decent house; have a good job; and a good education must be available for yourself and for your own children. On this whole issue, I once overheard a friend, in a moment of anger, saying to his daughter:

> If you are not careful, you will end up being a waitress, and make nothing of your life. Is that what you want to do for the rest of your life?

This father was well intentioned, but he was frustrated that his daughter had the potential to do something other than waiting at tables, which was her current part time job. He was finding it hard to motivate her into studying. But what he said reflected his innermost thoughts. He had graded the job as a waitress, as being one that ranked low on his list of suitable occupations. In his eyes it was demeaning for his daughter to stoop so low. This same father enjoyed dining out. When he did so he was waited upon in restaurants. He would tip those who waited upon him, quite generously. Ironically he wanted other people's daughters and sons to wait upon him, but he did not want his own daughter waiting upon others. What he was really saying to his daughter was:

> If you take this path, then in my eyes you will have failed. You will not go to university and you will have wasted all of the academic acumen that you have and you will end up in some dead end job for the rest of your life. That is failure, in my book, with a resounding 'F'.

I do not have time to go into this in more detail, but, I am a father myself (perhaps I am not that good a one at times), sometimes we have to kick ourselves and stop judging others by their occupation and the resulting level of wealth. Let me ask you a question. What would you define as being a good job? Or, let's go further. What would you define as a job that is detrimental and beneath you and your children? Now, think about your own definitions of categorising a job as being worthwhile and consider how you value someone who is doing that good job? Finally, how do you value someone who is engaged in a demeaning job?

Thinking out loud, would wiping the backside of someone, after they have been to the toilet be a demeaning job for you, or your child to perform (I am not talking nursing here)? Most of us would baulk at such a task. But what if I were to tell you that if you did this job, it would open up opportunities to power, wealth and influence over a nation. Would that be more interesting a proposition? What if you were given a title to go with this job. Say you were called: The Groom of the Stool. Is that enough for you? Not yet? Most would think this is a pretty bad job. Allow me to put it into context. King Henry VIII employed such a person. It was not the lowest of the low who normally hankered after the job of wiping the King's bum, it was his courtiers. If you were able to do this job you had time alone with the King. You could become a confidant of the King and you would have his ear on all sorts of policies. Does the job now appeal?

As another example of judging people by their occupation, it is worth recalling that Einstein's early career included the evaluation of patent applications for electromagnetic machines at the Swiss Patent Office. But, this genius was passed over for promotion until he was fully able to master machine based technology!

Jesus was a lowly carpenter. Look what happened there! We should take care before we pigeon hole people and classify people by their occupation and education, our adjudging that someone has an apparent lack of kudos in their job may be entirely misplaced. But, we do tend to associate a person's worth by their occupation. Through these assumptions we then place people that we meet into an income bracket. We then have a value tag in terms of wealth.

So now how rich do you think you are? This can be an uncomfortable question for many of us, especially if we live in the Western hemisphere. Before you answer this question we need to consider some of the statistics that are often bandied about, then we can attempt to establish, in material terms, just what being wealthy means. The answer is not as simple as one might think. It is generally acknowledged that there are two main methods of working out how wealthy we are, in world terms (I will not bore you with the details), depending upon which method is employed you can arrive at wildly varying figures.

You may have also heard such facts as: the average person in the world lives on just $1-$2 (U.S.) per day.[i] However, this figure can be arrived at by using a flawed format. For example, I live in the U.K., I have a mortgage, three children (who can be astonishingly expensive), a car, food to buy—normally from a supermarket—phone bills, water, gas electricity etc… A poor farmer in South America, Africa, Asia, or on the Indian sub continent might grow their own food rather than shop for it; furthermore they probably have no mortgage on their home, possibly no car

---

[i]For more on this please see: http://www.success-and-culture.net/articles/percapitaincome.shtml

that requires fuel etc… The immediate need for a larger level of income for such a farmer, may be proportionately far less than our own current lifestyle demands.

Before you howl at me and arrive at the conclusion that I am callous, please note that I am not advocating poverty. I prefer living in the U.K. by far, rather than Sub-Saharan Africa or in a remote region in Asia. I enjoy my home comforts— probably too much—and herein lies the problem. In a country of wealth we have managed to back ourselves into a corner. In order to sustain our lifestyle there is an accompanying need to maintain a certain level of income, which is always going to be higher than someone on the other side of the impoverished world. By using this as an illustration, I am trying to show that when arbitrary figures are used to demonstrate how rich one side of the world is, compared to another, they are, in my view, open to distortion. Let me elaborate upon this a little further with the following story:

When visiting a remote area of Kenya a dozen or so Westerners saw that a lady was living in a mud hut, as many do, but this was very different from most. This lady's house—I use the word "house" very loosely—had some form of dried grass, or straw, on the roof of her home with ever expanding holes in this crude arrangement. The building consisted of a solitary room with a mud floor.

Eventually there would be no roof and nowhere for the family to shelter under. Every time it rained, the water would pour in and it washed away a little more of the roof. The immediate need for this lady and her family was for a better, and more secure, form of accommodation to fulfil the basic need to be kept dry. The visitors from the U.K. enquired how much it would cost for a new roof to be built. For a few pounds (around £50 or £60—from memory) the material for a new corrugated metal roof could be bought. The cost of labour for the subsequent installation was also negligible. The visitors had a whip round, and they offered to pay for the materials and work. The local community heard of this offer. As word spread offers of help came in from the neighbours of this lady. One offered wood for the internal structure of a new house. Another offered to pay for the labour to construct the new home and to pay for the labour to source, mix and build the mud and dung walls. (It sounds salubrious, doesn't it? Do you want to live there?)

What do you think when reading of this generosity? Were the locals shamed into giving? Were the rich Westerners feeling so guilty that they gave cash to install a new roof? Were they wanting to assuage their guilt? It could have been a number of these issues. What if I were to tell you that the Kenyan community were part of a successful educational project that had commenced a few years earlier, a farm school initiative that is supported by many churches, and individuals, in the U.K. and beyond. The aim of this project is to help individual farmers to come together as a community, to help one another, to teach self sufficiency as a community and this project is transforming the area. The visiting Westerners were a few ordinary people, from the U.K. who saw the basic need of one person when visiting the project. They responded with a relatively small gift. This example of generosity motivated the local community to go one step further. In this instance the community had become infected with this attitude of giving and sacrifice. This story illustrates the point that the immediate needs of the farming lady were far less, in monetary terms, than those that we have come to expect (almost as a right) in the West. For example, if someone were homeless in the U.K. would you be able to build a two room bungalow for so little money? And what of the market value of this new house in the Rift Valley. If the property of wooden poles, mud and cow dung were located in my own town it would be worthless! This is a clear distortion of values. Let me ask another question. Was the farming lady now richer in any way? She had a new house, with two rooms instead of one; she was going to use her old house for cooking; and most importantly, both she and her family were now dry. In material terms she was far richer and her health was liable to improve. She had almost doubled the size of her living space. But let's go further. What is the cost comparison between the doubling in size of that lady's home and a typical three bed Edwardian terraced home in Harrow, North West London. How much would it cost? I outline the relevant—estimated—costs in the table opposite:

	Kenya	(Harrow) U.K.
Existing home value	£150.00	£300,000.00
New home value (when doubled)	£300.00	£600,000.00
Cost of monthly repayments—additional mortgage	£0.83 ($1.26 U.S. dollars)	£1,667.50 ($2,567.48 U.S. dollars)

The mortgage repayment figures are based upon a fixed interest rate of 4.5%, on a capital and interest repayment basis, over a period of 25 years, for loans of £150.00 and £300,000 respectively.

Would you be able to afford an extra £0.83 per month? I assume that most who live in the U.K. probably would be able to do so (I acknowledge that some may not be able to afford even this). Would you be able to afford an additional £1,667.50 every month, for the next 25 years? I assume that having to make these payments would have some form of impact on most of our lives. But, the increase—in percentage terms—of the size of both properties, would be the same, as both properties would have been doubled in size. Let's take this one step further by examining the average Per-Capita-Income[ii] levels in the U.K., and in Kenya, as follows:

	Annual Per-Capita-Income
Kenya	$315.04 (U.S. dollars)
U.K.	$24,486.70 (U.S. dollars)
World Average	$5,737.28 (U.S. dollars)

These figures are very hard to ascertain. The information available for this varies quite markedly.

From this we can see—in material terms—by living in the U.K. we enjoy an average income that is well above the world average, and far above that of the average for someone living in Kenya.

Now let's see how much of the respective Per-Capita-Income levels would be used on the mortgages that I have outlined at the top of this page:

[ii] Per-Capita-Income is the amount each citizen of a country would receive if the yearly national income of that same country is divided equally among the entire population.

	Utilisation of Income
Kenya	$1.26 x 12 months = $15.12
	15.12 / 315.04 = 4.79% of income
U.K.	$2,567.48 x 12 months = $30,809.76
	30,809.76 / 24,486.70 = 125.82% of income

Percentages are rounded. I also realise that gaining a mortgage at 100% of the value of a property extension is virtually impossible, today. U.S.$ are used as they are the most accurate figures for Per-Capita-Income.

These calculations demonstrate that to double the size of the respective properties, and if someone in Kenya took out a mortgage as shown, the repayments would eat up 4.79% of Per-Capita-Income. For someone living in the U.K. it would be a ludicrously high percentage that is greater than the average Per-Capita-Income of the U.K.!

I am aware of the saying that there are lies, damn lies and statistics, but I hope that this exercise demonstrates the point that declaring arbitrary monetary figures in order to rank wealth by each country, on a global scale, is, in reality, much more of a relative matter than it might appear to be on the surface.

I emphasise that it is NOT right that some of us live with clean running water, sanitation, more than enough food, clothing etc…when so many others have so very little or no access to all of these utilities. But, if everyone enjoyed the same standard of living that many of us in the West enjoy the cost of living would inevitably increase, significantly. On the one hand many of us want to see more equality across the globe and a reduction in poverty, but would we really be prepared to pay a lot more for our: car; TV; radio; washing machine; oven and hob; kitchen fixtures and fittings; bedroom furniture; food; most of the clothes that we wear, right down to our pants and knickers?

The vast majority of goods that people living in the West enjoy, are often manufactured cheaply overseas, or at least the parts that make up these goods are very cheap, such as: microchips; dyes for clothing; glues that hold stuff together. If everyone attained the extremely honourable dream of material equality the salaries of workers in poorer countries would have to increase. Many of us would no longer be able to afford the basics. Would there be some form of economic adjustment downwards in the cost of manufacture? What is known is that suddenly our world would be transformed financially. Quite how, no one really knows. Equality of wealth has never been in existence on earth, since man was banished from the Garden of Eden.

A remarkable preacher and Rabbi, called Yeshua (Jesus), whilst living and wandering about in first century Palestine said this:

I tell you the truth, it is hard for a rich man to enter the kingdom of heaven.[iii]

The kingdom of heaven, in the Holy Bible, is portrayed (among other things) as a place of equality, with no suffering or pain, a place of justice and peace. How closely does your own life, with all the accompanying trinkets of wealth, correlate to being a life of equality, justice and peace?

Take a moment to consider your own possessions. Do you own a: mobile phone; computer; TV; hi-fi; alarm clock etc…? In your kitchen do you have a: dish washer (apart your wife—lol); washing machine (again, apart from your wife—more lol); vacuum cleaner; oven; hob; microwave? Do you enjoy a: power shower; flushing toilet; central heating? What about outside your home? Do you have: a lawn mower; a strimmer; a hedge cutter; a car? Think about the clothes that you wear and the periphery of: your jewellery; your watch etc… How would you feel if you could no longer afford any of these possessions?

Living in the West many of us have gained a level of lifestyle of what we perceive to be within the scope of our needs, but our Western lifestyle is well beyond the comprehension, or the imagining, of a farmer in a remote backwater in the continent of Africa. We now have an inherent desire and an expectation to have all of this stuff and this expectation maintains the current status quo of the smaller Western population of the world being supplied with everything that one could possibly want, whilst the far larger populace of the rest of our planet continues to live in abject poverty!

Do you watch programmes such as: Dragons Den? You may know the sort of

---

[iii] The Gospel of Matthew, Chapter 19, verse 23.

thing. It is where someone pitches an idea and they need funding to bring their idea to fruition. Wealthy entrepreneurs sit there with their vast amounts of cash for all to see, piled up on tables in front of each millionaire. An inventor might come onto this show and they pitch for the money that they need to get production underway for their invention. More often than not the budding inventor wants to get their product manufactured in the Far East because there is cheap labour available. There appears to be little investigation or concern as to the working conditions in these far off lands by the inventor or the potential investors. What of the rights of the workers, do they have any? What of the working practices? Is a fair wage being paid to these employees? This is before we even consider general human rights abuses in say China, Burma, Indonesia etc... If the rich entrepreneur likes what they see—sometimes—one of the main deciding factors that will clinch the deal and the subsequent investment of capital, is the cost of production. Inevitably the entrepreneurs enquire: How cheap is it to manufacture and package each unit? Did you hear that resounding echo across the globe—and into the highest of the heavens—the demeaning of God's ultimate creation? Do you hear the crass clanging when an individual is valued by how cheaply they can operate a machine that will make, assemble and package a solitary unit of an inventor? (Please note this is not a personal attack upon these good folk, whether they be inventor or investor, I use it just as an example. We do not see what goes on behind the scenes of these programmes, the inventors and entrepreneurs may be some of the most ethical people on the planet.)

But wait, before we sit in harsh judgement upon these venture capitalists, ask this question. Who is it that buys that invention, once it is in production and on display in our shops? It is you and me, my friend, it is you and me. We are happy to be part of this global machine. When we buy all of our: white goods; cars; electrical gadgets; we want to buy them cheaply. We may march on governments, or attend a summit on poverty, shouting and holding placards up for change, but how much do we really care for the needs and the rights of those who manufacture these goods, or the bits and pieces that go inside them? Perhaps the far bigger question is, should we give a damn? I sometimes wonder what will happen at the day of judgement:

> [34]"Then the King will say to those on his right, 'Come, you who are blessed by my Father; take your inheritance, the kingdom prepared for you since the creation of the world. [35]For I was hungry and you gave me something to eat, I was thirsty and you gave me something to drink, I was a stranger and you invited me in, [36]I needed clothes and you clothed me, I was sick and you looked after me, I was in prison and you came to visit me.'
>
> [37]"Then the righteous will answer him, 'Lord, when did we see you hungry and feed you, or thirsty and give you something to drink? [38]When did we see you a stranger and invite you in, or needing clothes and clothe you? [39]When did we see you sick or in prison and go to visit you?'
>
> [40]"The King will reply, 'I tell you the truth, whatever you did for one of the least of these brothers of mine, you did for me.'
>
> [41]"Then he will say to those on his left, 'Depart from me, you who are cursed, into the eternal fire prepared for the devil and his angels. [42]For I was hungry and you gave me nothing to eat, I was thirsty and you gave me nothing to drink, [43]I was a stranger and you did not invite me in, I needed clothes and you did not clothe me, I was sick and in prison and you did not look after me.'
>
> [44]"They also will answer, 'Lord, when did we see you hungry or thirsty or a stranger or needing clothes or sick or in prison, and did not help you?'
>
> [45]"He will reply, 'I tell you the truth, whatever you did not do for one of the least of these, you did not do for me.'
>
> [46]"Then they will go away to eternal punishment, but the righteous to eternal life."

This text is from the Bible and the gospel of Matthew and Chapter 25. After reading this would you consider yourself as being righteous? Are you worried? If you do not believe in eternal life I suppose that you will not worry much. But, for those of us who adhere to faith, how do we square our belief in God's justice with our participation in this global machine? On the one hand, we should be feeding and clothing the poverty stricken, but most of us are almost certainly participants in keeping many in poverty through our purchasing decisions.

Regarding the whole arena of Per-Capita-Income, I used to take figures about income levels as being gospel. I have changed my mind somewhat when considering the enormity of this dilemma. I acknowledge that there is poverty—and this is an utterly shameful and evil position in a world of plenty. I must also acknowledge that I am in a privileged position. I try, therefore, to do what I can. I look to buying fair trade, when possible, and if affordable. I try to look into the origin of some larger items, such as dining room tables, white goods etc… I try to support smaller businesses in my own home town, rather than the huge conglomerates. My business recycles everything that it can, and we recycle at home (not because of global warming—I feel the science could go either way on this one—I recycle because it appears to be good stewardship to do so). I buy fuel for my car that has less emissions, when affordable. Occasionally I will write to my MP and those in authority, even the prime minister on rare occasions. I have also learned to pray more.

I have also reviewed my own charitable giving. In the main I support charities that I can get involved in, read about and pray for. I know the people running these charities, on a local level, and I can see where the money goes. I might give—on an ad-hoc basis—to other charities if there is a disaster in the world. But, despite what I have said, I don't go around feeling guilty about world poverty. I do not say this as some pseudo saint, wanting to appear self-righteous or above anyone else, I am merely outlining what has helped me to come to terms with my own wealth in trying to deal with some of the poverty that I see in the world at large.

I continue to be extremely saddened that in a world of plenty we continue to see extreme poverty, but guilt achieves nothing. Sometimes the enormity of the situation and the guilt that we feel can result in inaction as the problems of wealth v poverty is so huge, seemingly it cannot be solved, and so we do little as we do not know where to begin on tackling such a big problem. I am also past the stage of feeling that wealth is wrong, something to be shunned.

However, I have arrived at this very unhappy position of balance after much searching, prayer and contemplation. I have not got all of the answers sewn up and my solution is not ideal, of course it isn't, but it really is the best I can think of in our modern day global market.

I have explained, in my introduction that the Holy Bible is my final arbitrator in all matters. At this point I would like to explore some of these conundrums from what I believe to be a Biblical perspective and how these have affected my thought process.

Firstly, I become uncomfortable when Christians start to talk of wealth as being unhealthy. I cannot find anywhere in the scriptures that being wealthy is wrong.

By contrast I abhor poverty and the abuse of any workforce, but globally I can do nothing about this, but this should not prevent me from wanting to do something. A paradox I know, but...

I believe that the Holy Bible clearly teaches that we are to care for the poor and when we find ourselves in a position of power and wealth, we are to throw far more than a begrudging meagre lifeline, or guilt offering, to those who are struggling.

When I read the Old Testament[iv] I discover that the people of God are taught, time and time again, to look after the alien, the poor, the widowed, the orphan, the dispossessed. This is a basic tenet of the instructions given by God to his chosen people as an example of what marked them out as being different from the nations around them. This indicates that the nature of mankind, thousands of years ago, was much the same as today. God had to instruct his people in a social relief programme as there must have been little social care in place for the afflicted and poor at the time.

I believe that the Holy Bible contrasts the attitude of man with the mind of a God of ultimate holiness and purity. Let's consider some examples by starting with the book within the Holy Bible called Deuteronomy, and look at Chapter 15 and

---

[iv] This is a section of the Holy Bible that is divided into different books. The Old Testament records the journey of these people, their poetry, songs, and instructions that many believe were given by God.

verse 7. This is just one example where God's chosen people are instructed, by God, to be generous to the poor:

> …do not be tight fisted.[v]

I also look to Deuteronomy, Chapter 24 and verses 19 to 21:

> [19]When you are harvesting in your field and you overlook a sheaf, do not go back to get it. Leave it for the alien, the fatherless and the widow, so that the LORD your God may bless you in all the work of your hands. [20]When you beat the olives from your trees, do not go over the branches a second time. Leave what remains for the alien, the fatherless and the widow. [21]When you harvest the grapes in your vineyard, do not go over the vines again. Leave what remains for the alien, the fatherless and the widow.

In these verses—and many others—the people are told, by God, to leave the surplus harvest that falls to the ground, or the remains of the trees and the vine for the poverty stricken who live among them. These instructions resound with: do not be greedy for on the earth and from the harvest there is enough for both you and for the poor. How would I apply this to the society that we live in, particularly in the relative comfort of the West?

Firstly, the provision of the created order in the world is sufficient for all, a more even distribution of resources and wealth is required. I cannot influence this in any major way. But, as I have said, in all of the Biblical references that I have read I do not see a condemnation of wealth in itself by God (I cannot say this enough). What I read is a continual plea—by our mighty, divine and loving God—for those with plenty to change their attitudes. The wealthy are to be liberators of the poor in society. (When I look at the fortunes made by the few in the global markets I believe that our society lives well outside of this remit.)

For most of us we do not live off the land in as direct a manner as an Israelite

---

[v] For an extensive list of references in the Bible, please go to: http://home.snu.edu/~hculbert/poor.htm

farmer and I imagine that most farmers of today would not take too kindly to us wandering through their fields of corn, helping ourselves to the harvest, or even nicking the odd pig or cow from a field. Such actions may result in the local constabulary being summoned. The supermarkets appear to have a surplus amount of food that is nearing, or past, its sell by or best before date. A Godly practice, today, would be the supermarket chains, throughout the land, alleviating poverty by taking the radical step of throwing open their doors and engaging in a policy of allowing the poor and dispossessed to come into a store, after closing time, to help themselves, gratis to this almost out of date food! Wouldn't this be an astoundingly liberating act for our society?

But then again, I wonder, in a society of self-centredness how this would work? On the one hand would the poor be too embarrassed, or too proud, to claim free food? Would many, who are not really poor, simply go in and help themselves anyway? I suspect that it would be a combination of the two.

So here is an alternative for you Mr. Sainsbury, Mr. Tesco, Mr. Asda, Mr. Waitrose, Mr. Morrison and co. I challenge you to give away all food and produce that is nearing its sell by date, or best before date, to local charities who distribute food to the homeless and destitute[vi] in our villages, towns and cities from Lands End to John O'Groats. Will you commit to this rather than throwing away perfectly edible food each day? Why not be generous, give it away (if you don't already)? I cannot see why this policy could not be bought in by the supermarket chains, more or less over-night. Wouldn't this start to transform our society here in the U.K.? Perhaps what prevents this type of business practice being widespread is what the first century Rabbi named Yeshua (Jesus) talked about within his teaching. In the gospel of Matthew, and Chapter 6, he states that:

> [24]No one can serve two masters. Either he will hate the one and love the other, or he will be devoted to the one and despise the other. You cannot serve both God and Money.

[vi]Allegedly—according to friend of mine—a well known store did do this, but they were sued by a homeless person when they suffered an allergic reaction to the free food donated to a charity by a supermarket. I am certain that some fair distribution system could be worked out.

The apostle, that we call Paul, expands upon this theme in his first letter to Timothy, in Chapter 6 with:

> ¹⁰For the love of money is a root of all kinds of evil. Some people, eager for money, have wandered from the faith and pierced themselves with many griefs.

Please note that it is not wealth, or money in itself is labelled as being the root of all evil. The root of all evil is a possessive attitude towards commodities, possessions and a general desire for wealth. If we find comfort and reassurance from all that we own and possess, we must acknowledge that such comfort is bound to be transitory. Like the Israelite farmer with their crops, it takes a deliberate effort of will to treat all that we have as mere trinkets and of no real value. This does not mean that we should treat what we own with contempt, the Holy Bible clearly teaches us that we are stewards, and as such we should be responsible with what we have. Furthermore we must not begrudge or judge those with wealth.[vii]

All of this relates to our perception of what wealth is for. Is it all for our own gain, or is it for us and the wider community, and as such, have we a responsibility when using and deploying our wealth? The Biblical message is that we will be judged by a higher power as to how we have used and distributed our own wealth. Whether you believe this or not, is up to you. Threats of damnation should not be the sole motivator for our own charitable actions.

Though being wealthy is not an inherent sin there are very many traps into which we can fall and the dangers of wealth lie within ourselves. What threatens our very soul is what we desire and lust after and this is the primary concern of the God that I know, love and try to serve.

As I have said, if we do not adopt a healthy (if somewhat compromising) attitude to wealth, then we can go around feeling guilty and morose. This is what was

---

[vii] Please read in the book of Matthew, Chapter 7, about judging others. We can judge, but we must do this with great caution.

happening in the following situation:

> A friend of mine explained to me that they felt ever so guilty about their wealth. Their husband had a well paid job, they were upper middle class, quite well off, almost too well off she felt.
>
> Another friend had recommended that they sponsor a child in the developing world overseas.
>
> The reply came: I do that already, I sponsor five children.

I would be presumptuous in suggesting that this lady was caught in a cycle of guilt because she had not learned how to handle wealth, but her attitude within herself, was revealed by the vocalisation of her guilt to more than one person. It obviously bugged her, despite her generosity in supporting children overseas. My suggestion, at the time, was simple; give more, and the guilt would disappear. But nothing is so easy, especially when dealing with emotions.

Today, I would not offer this as a solution. I would ask questions such as: Why do you feel guilty? Are you able to be thankful for what you have been given? Are you saving and putting money to one side for the years of drought and hardship as a good steward? Are you saving for your own retirement? Are you taking individual responsibility seriously? Why do you give money away in the first place? What is your motivation? How involved are you in finding out about how your gifts of money are spent? Do you pray for those that you give money to? If so how often? There would be many other questions, too many to list here. Throwing money at charitable works is not the answer to assuaging our guilt.

Much of what we do, to relieve poverty is well intentioned, but I am becoming more and more amused at the facebook messages of friends inviting me to badger a politician about some issue or other. Does this achieve anything? How easy is it to click a computer button and leave it there, believing that we have done something to alleviate poverty and justice? Taking so little action is simply passive inadequacy. If sending a protest via a social networking page is part of a structured campaign, fair enough, but if this is all that you are doing, then don't expect anything to change.

If facebook had been around in the day of the great reformer William Wilberforce, hands up who thinks that just clicking a button would have changed the course of human history? It took conviction, tireless campaigning, enormous amounts of energy and sacrifice over many years—with a little skulduggery—to gain the abolition of the trade in human beings. (The most shameful legacy is that it is reckoned that there are more slaves today than there ever were—allegedly around 40% of the cocoa bean is reckoned to be harvested by slaves, I see no facebook campaign on this issue. Is this because we all like chocolate so much?)

I see in scripture a concern for the state of our hearts and minds, by our creator God. As I have mentioned, many people cite the fact that money and wealth is one of the most often mentioned topics of the Holy Bible, this is true, but I don't believe that it is the physical amount of wealth that is of primary concern to God, it is our attitude toward this wealth.

God, as evidenced in the Holy Bible, continually examines the heart of mankind and he requires the deliberate engaging of our minds to change our mindset. Our words and actions display what is within us, deep within. It is a delicate balance and it is something that is hard to achieve, I still struggle with all of this, please find your own path. Feel free to let me know if it is any better than my own.

Earlier I commented that I prefer to live in the U.K. as opposed to living in poverty in Africa. I would also like to clarify one important point before we pat ourselves on the back, as we manage to justify the need for wealth. As I have illustrated earlier, there is one major difference between the farmer in Kenya and ourselves. It is one of choice. I have the choice whether I live in a house valued at around £300,000 or a property valued for less. For many of us, our position is something that cannot be bought, or saved for, it is by a thankful accident of birth that many of us are born into this privileged position of having these choices. The farmer in Kenya has no real choice. They are living in a mud hut due to the circumstances of their birth, and they have no virtually no chance of ever getting out of such a position. (Many who live in the West also have little choice.)

I believe that many of us in the West need to reassess our own position of making choices, quite radically. What has happened in society and within the financial markets, is that we forgot to leave the metaphorical sheaves of corn on the ground, for collection by the poor. Until now, we have wanted to keep the entire harvest for ourselves. Those on big bonuses wanted to acquire more and more of the harvest. We have seen some city financiers become selfish, wealthy and insular. But these attitudes and the acquisition of wealth was not confined only to the so called Bankers. More on this as we progress through this book.

Having visited a relief project in Maseno, in Kenya, I would wish to bring clarification to another point. I much prefer the health care available in the West, I prefer living in the climate that I do—especially with my fair skin that burns easily under the rays of the sun—I enjoy having a nice comfortable car, I like the fact that I live an area that is relatively free of crime, I am grateful that I can shop for what I require easily, I love having a TV, reliable Internet access, a constant supply of electricity, gas and clean drinking water, I have virtually no chance of contracting cholera. The list of the basics—and luxury items—available to me is almost endless. But with such a lifestyle at my disposal, why do I pine for my friends in Kenya? Why do I have to hold back my tears when leaving there, every single time? Why do I want to go back there again and again? I hunger, literally hunger, for my next trip, why? Why have I seriously considered living there? I look forward to travelling there, living on comparatively meagre rations, driving around rut infested mud lanes that shake every single bone in my body to visit farmers and orphans. But why, again I ask why? It is because most of these poor farmers have nothing and yet, many have more than I can imagine. Certainly many have an amazing faith in God, but leaving that to one side, they value everything that they possess.

Many in the West, within this economic crisis, have only come to value their possessions because they are in danger of losing them with the ability to acquire more. It has taken a dramatic financial crisis for this to come about. But this valuing of posesssions is not due to a realignment of values to being more altruistic, it is a selfish anxiety that our stuff might disappear down the Swanny and many of us just want to keep hold of it all!

Our churches are not immune to these attitudes, for in contrast to the endemic faith and extreme reliance upon God—that I have witnessed in Kenya—many of us in today's Western church might sing lines such as:

> I surrender all, I surrender all;
> All to thee, my blessed Saviour,
> I surrender all…

Once we have raised our hands in the air—singing such songs of praise—and after declaring fervently that yes God, we give everything to you; we hear a sermon that is good and thought provoking; this might motivate us to go forward for prayer ministry; we have a cup of coffee and a nice chat; then we go back to our houses; to enjoy a lovely meal, perhaps with family and friends. There is nothing intrinsically wrong with all of this structure, but life, or what we perceive to be our real day to day life, then continues as normal almost divorced from what we have sung, heard and responded to. Let's not kid ourselves, have we really surrendered our all and everything to God, especially financially?

In the West we have spiritualised our church life as our Christian concept of sacrifice and surrender tends to relate almost solely to our inner self and our hearts. This submission is good, but so very little of our lives really extend as a seamless act of worship through the week. Little of most of our daily lives relates to giving up anything of our material possessions, save the money that goes out from our bank account—to the church—each month. If we look at the financial hub of each country, we can see the wealth, or at least perceive it, but there is little to do with worship and sacrifice to God within the structures of the global market place.

For example, in the gospel of Luke, Chapter 18, there is the following account of a rich young ruler:

> [18]A certain ruler asked him, "Good teacher, what must I do to inherit eternal life?"
>
> [19]"Why do you call me good?" Jesus answered. "No one is good—except God alone. [20]You know the commandments: 'Do not commit adultery, do

not murder, do not steal, do not give false testimony, honour your father and mother.'"

²¹"All these I have kept since I was a boy," he said.

²²When Jesus heard this, he said to him, "You still lack one thing. Sell everything you have and give to the poor, and you will have treasure in heaven. Then come, follow me."

²³When he heard this, he became very sad, because he was a man of great wealth. ²⁴Jesus looked at him and said, "How hard it is for the rich to enter the kingdom of God! ²⁵Indeed, it is easier for a camel to go through the eye of a needle than for a rich man to enter the kingdom of God."

I have heard many comment upon this account and the strange thing is, to a man, the preacher has always pointed up the social scale, away from themselves and their congregation when talking of the rich young ruler. We find it far easier to point the accusing finger away from ourselves. We rarely cast ourselves in the role of the rich young man for there are always others who are richer than us and this message is for them we say. So it is with the banking crisis. It is the rich who are responsible, not us. We are divorced from the cause. But are we? Are we really blameless as a corporate society? To view this parable as being about ourselves is far too scary. If we did, then we too might be asked to give up everything and follow, I mean really follow, Yeshua (Jesus) (or our own moral path). Let's keep the idea of giving up everything that I have at arms length, that is for someone else, perhaps the Bankers, but it is not for me! When we sing of surrender and giving in the churches of the land, let's stick to our inner soul, we are fairly comfortable with that and all of the nice gooey emotion that accompanies such Surrender!

I have come to realise that we Western Christians are almost spiritually schizophrenic. Many of us are willing to stand surrendering and rejoicing in church on a Sunday, which in itself is good, but when we return to our homes we continue to watch the same trashy TV, rather than pray; we continue to overeat and drink without giving thanks to God for his provision—when was the last time you prayed before a meal in a public restaurant?

If we are to live up to the real call of the church this all needs to be considered carefully. Perhaps we might consider opening up our homes for lunch for the alcoholic; the drug user; the prostitute; the homeless guy; those in debt; those going through divorce; those who are fighting for rights to see their children when their marriage has broken down; or perhaps it is the lonely nutter who sits in church each week whom no-one really talks too, I agree, they are hard work, perhaps all they need is a friend to talk to and to show them some kindness. Once we do this, and more, then we might learn sacrifice and surrender and then, and only then, can we really look to the wealthy Bankers and say do likewise. We in the church should be the example to those who work in the world of finance. I am doubtful as to whether we in the church are that good an example, and so our voice on many other issues is impotent.

Whilst we live in the West in a position of relative wealth that is well above that of a poor farmer in Africa, what gives us the right to lecture anyone else on riches? That poor farmer could as easily lecture us. That is some of what I think Yeshua (Jesus) was talking about when he says be very careful before judging others. Whatever plumb line you use, it will be used against you! So be very careful.

By the way, I am not lecturing anyone here, I am on this journey with you and I need to learn this as much as anyone, but if we are calling ourselves Christian, we need to constantly ask ourselves, do we really imitate Christ? Is your church anything like the church that Christ came to establish, really, honestly? Aren't we in danger of committing perjury in much of what we sing, pray and say, week by week in our churches up and down this land? And yet we dare to speak of, and hold out for an expectation of some form of revival!

This language of sacrifice, surrender, worship and grace is probably alien to most who work in the city but that does not make them bad people. Misguided, some of them may be, but inherently and intentionally bad…? I would question whether this is endemic. (I know of many financiers who support charitable work with vast sums of money, let alone the amount of tax they pay as individuals and companies.)

More of this as we progress.

Let me begin to close this chapter with a story that illustrates what it is to really surrender all. A story that I hope we can all learn from. This account comes from my second home in Kenya:

> An orphaned boy was holding in his hand five small grains, from a roasted cob of corn. This is a rare treat for an orphan. The moment that he appeared at an orphan feeding station, he was swamped by around twenty fellow orphans. He willingly passed out all but one grain to his friends, who clamoured for a taste of just one grain in the melee. One by one he distributed the grains by sharing in his feast. He retained a solitary grain for himself.
>
> Then his best friend—who had been playing some distance away—came running up and he pushed to the front. There were no grains left to share, just the small remaining grain of corn. Still the best friend asked if he could have this little grain of roasted cob for himself. (We can walk into any supermarket in the land and buy a whole cob, and bake it in an oven, but to these orphans owning anything of a roasted cob is so far beyond their reach.)
>
> The orphan who held that solitary grain hesitated, finally he acceded to the request of his best mate.
>
> This young barefooted orphan generously gave up all of the grains that he held as a token of his friendship. To him, apart from the torn shirt upon his back and the ragged shorts that he wore, it was all that he possessed in the world. He gave up the chance to partake of a banquet. He gave up everything. Unlike most of us, he could have truly sung, with no fear of perjuring himself: I surrender all!

Would I do the same, would you give up your absolute all, if required of you? What is the equivalent for all of us, whether we be a Banker or an ordinary Joe? Imagine what giving up all that we have would be like? Could you do it? I would suggest that for us, our giving up everything would be very hard to do. We have far bigger stuff to lose than a few grains of corn.

This concept of sacrifice strikes at the very centre of our hearts, and thus the heart of the problem (and the heart of the credit and banking crisis—more of this as we progress through this book). An orphan in a small, unknown and unremarkable town, set in the huge continent of Africa, with a few meagre grains of corn can teach us so much about self-sacrifice. This lack of sacrifice is, I believe at the heart of the current economic woes that we face. For on the opposite side of the spectrum is selfishness.

So how rich are you, in world terms? This is the question that I posed toward beginning of this chapter. The answer is complex, generally we might be wealthy in a material sense, but in reality are we poor? As a society we tend to treat possessions with utter disregard, merely as commodities that can be disposed of, discarded when they no longer serve our purpose and when we have no use for them; or if they are worn out, we can go out and buy a replacement. We may have to work hard for what we own, perhaps too hard; ignoring family values and those that we love. There is material poverty in this country, we should be utterly shamefaced that in this great country of ours—with so much wealth at our disposal—there continues to be such abject poverty, but there are other forms of poverty. Our children are impoverished of time with their parents; relationships are impoverished as they break down; families are torn apart and rent asunder. Poverty comes in different forms to a lack of material wealth.

In closing this first chapter, I firmly believe that it does not matter how materially wealthy we are, it is our attitude towards this material wealth that is of primary importance. Once we allow God's grace to perform open heart surgery upon us and our financial institutions, perhaps then we will have a chance of rediscovering what real wealth is.

I also believe that the financial sectors, worldwide, have suffered a massive coronary heart attack. Drastic surgery is required, a triple bypass is what the surgeon in our heaven prescribes and that we, the ultimate of his creation, are stewards. Our economies are sick, they maybe on the verge of death, perhaps in their death throes in their current form. In fact, we might just lose everything anyway, sometime soon. The following is an extract from a report by Paul Thompson and it can be found on the Daily Mail online site. It is dated 6th March 2009:

>A century and a half ago it was at the centre of the Californian gold rush, with hopeful prospectors pitching their tents along the banks of the American River.
>
>Today, tents are once again springing up in the city of Sacramento. But this time it is for people with no hope and no prospects.
>
>With America's economy in free fall and its housing market in crisis, California's state capital has become home to a tented city for the dispossessed.
>
>Those who have lost their jobs and homes and have nowhere else to go are constructing makeshift shelters on the site, which covers several acres.
>
>As many as 50 people a week are turning up and the authorities estimate that the tent city is now home to more than 1,200 people.
>
>In a state more known for its fantastic wealth and the glitz and glamour of Hollywood, the images have shocked many Americans.
>
>Conditions are primitive, with no water supply or proper sanitation.
>
>Many residents have to walk up to three miles to buy bottled water from petrol stations or convenience stores.
>
>…As America's most powerful state California had the same gross domestic output as Italy and Spain, but it has been among the hardest hit by the recession and housing crisis.
>
>Foreclosure rates last year rocketed by 327% , with up to 500 people a day losing their home.
>
>…with no new home builds and as many as 80,000 people losing their job every month, there is little chance of employment.

Imagine what it would be like to live in a tent outside this glitzy town. No job, no sanitation, no water, no food. You are on the outside looking in at the wealth of celebrities and society at large. You have little hope of ever working again. For anyone to believe that they are immune within this crisis is vanity. When we examine the 1929 Wall St Crash we will see that that crisis hit every sector and strata of society irrelevant of status. So it is today. What is happening in California could happen to you in your own town or city.

The crisis facing the world has not been caused by the one sector of society, the Bankers, the cause lies at the door of our corporate society. We are also, all of us, part of the solution. So we need to reassess our own hearts and our expectations.

The financial markets may have lost sight of this decades ago, but the rest of us in society permitted it to happen. As long as the markets and our houses rose in value, no one—not even the regulators—batted an eyelid at our rapid accumulation of wealth. It became the accepted norm as did an easy line of credit. More on all of this later.

But prior to this crisis the faith communities stayed fairly silent. I believe that many of us Christians were too busy spiritualising life. We moved away from the Biblical principles of valuing one another, instead we valued our stuff far too much. We lost sight of being created in the very image of God. Because of these losses our care for the poor and the dispossessed did not matter to most of us. Many of us—Banker, politician, regulator, faith leaders, ordinary Joe—were all too busy gathering in the entire harvest for ourselves to notice what was going wrong.

Once we have re-discovered the call of God and when we have got down onto our knees and begged for HIS anointing within our social and financial infrastructure, greed will dissipate, as will any form of judgement, jealousy, pride, arrogance and all of the other emotions that I have touched upon, once we re-learn surrender, sacrifice and social justice, then, and only then, might we have a slim chance of becoming like that orphan, who was prepared to give up everything, thereby enabling others to experience a momentary feast of pleasure that revolved around a small insignificant roasted piece of maize!

Are you prepared to embark upon this journey of discovery and potential sacrifice? If you are not, then I advise you to wait, retreat and simply cross your fingers and hope against hope that the financial tsunami that may yet hit us will pass you by.

CHAPTER TWO

HE STARTED IT

The media has dedicated a vast amount of copy in their reporting upon the credit crunch and the accompanying banking crisis. Much of the blame for all that has gone wrong has been laid firmly and squarely at the door of the Bankers. They have been—and they continue to be—labelled as being avaricious. The list of grudges that many hold against them is almost endless.

Are you one of those people who get worked up and angry when you read and hear headlines about Bankers and their bonuses? Are you upset that so few people could gain so much in the way of bonuses? Do you think it wrong that they earn so much? Do you wonder why, when we as taxpayers own the banks, the bonus culture is not more restricted? No doubt you have experienced some, or all of these emotions.

In this chapter, and I am not defending anyone here—well I am sort of, but please don't shoot the messenger—I want to look at who this mysterious figure called a Banker is. I would also like to consider who owns the banks as this may bring some clarity to the nature of this blame game.

To try and answer some of the questions about Bankers let's delve right in and firstly consider, who does own the banks?

It has often been bandied around that we, the taxpayers now own the banks due to the recent bailout strategy. According to this definition, if you are a higher rate taxpayer does this mean that you own a bigger slice of the banks than a basic rate taxpayer? I also wonder where this leaves non-taxpayers? Do they own nothing of the banks as they pay no tax? Do Bankers, as taxpayers, employ themselves? The sweeping allegation that taxpayers own the banks raises so very many questions.

I am going to stick my neck out and say that both you and I own the banks in same the measure that you and I own the army; Royal Navy; RAF; police; doctors; nurses; social workers; teachers; prison warders; fire service; paramedics; and all of the state run departments and facilities, in their entirety.

Allow me to explain. Assume that I have some money in my own bank account. I clear out my bank account and I give all my money to a charity. Does this action mean that I now own a piece of the receiving charity? Do I now have a say over how that charity can spend the money that I have gifted to them? The reality is that I have no control over this gift as I no longer own the money. It has left my bank account, the trustees of the charity can utilise the gift that I have passed over to them as they see fit.

It is similar with the tax that I pay, save for a couple of differences, that I will cover in a moment. I go to work, I earn money, the government gains money from me, by taxing my income. Once the government have collected money from me, it is theirs, not mine. I have no choice as to how they spend the taxes that they have gained from me. I have no say over the sending of troops to war; how many teachers are employed; how many staff they engage to work in the NHS; whether they build a prison, school or hospital; whether they clean the streets or leave them dirty; the decision making process is not mine to make. I have zero power and no say as to how politicians spend taxes collected from me.

When the government decides to spend the taxes collected from us to purchase banking shares, they own these shares, not you or I. We, as taxpayers, legally own nada in the way of banking shares.

Earlier I said that there were some differences between my giving to a charitable cause and the collection of taxes, the first is that charities do not generally issue shares, and secondly, I choose to give to a charity, whereas the government collects taxes from me as a consequence of my living in the U.K. The one transaction is made of my own free will, the other is compulsory.

Once we get over this hurdle of who owns what, we can start to view the ownership of banks in an entirely different light. As we have no control over banking shares that are owned by the government, we must acknowledge that we have no say as to how, as an employer, they choose to run the banks. We cannot appoint people to the board of directors of these various banks. We will not be able to control how much in the manner of bonuses should be awarded to employees of a bank. I hope that you see the principle here. As taxpayers we cannot impose anything upon any of these financial institutions. However, this does makes things both easier and harder. It is easier as we cannot be held to account for the manner in which the banks are being run. But, it is also harder as we may be filled with frustration that nothing appears to change. From the media we gain the impression that the fat cats are continuing to get ever fatter. I would venture to suggest that getting frustrated and angry—in itself—achieves nothing of any substantial worth. Perhaps we would be better to let our feelings of anger subside. Alternatively we could write to our politicians and hold them to account (Do you see what I did there—we are talking about banks and I said that we could hold them to account, get it? It's laugh a minute with me.)

I would place a caveat upon all of this. The amount of government money that has been used to bail out the banks is staggering, it runs into billions of pounds. This might fill us with incredulity, I agree that it should never have been allowed to get to this point, but before we go off on one, we need to acknowledge that we cannot change the past, but it is worth pausing to consider what alternatives to this mass bail out were available at the time.

Firstly we need to consider the issue of dependency across the financial institutions. Banks lend to each other, in one form or another. Some of these loans are highly complex. I do not intend to go over the mind numbingly boring details, but there was—and there still is—a chain of loans that link the institutions to one another.

If a bank, let's call it: the Bank of Timbucto goes under, then, just like any other business, they will fail to honour their debts. If they cannot honour their obligations then the other banks such as a fictitious Bank of Wales, are not going to be paid what is owed to them by the defaulting Bank. In turn, when the Bank of Wales cannot meet their repayments, the banks of: HBOG; Talifax; Floyds; Pat-West and the bank of Slovakia, are not going to receive the money owed to them as they have all leant money to one another. This chain continues around a country, or region, and the repercussions of a defaulting bank (or government) may be felt all around the world. The effect can be like a financial tsunami, devastating everything that is standing in its path as the disastrous domino effect plays out.

This chain reaction has the potential to result in the total, and utter, collapse of retail and investment banking, throughout the world (not just the developed world) unless someone steps in, as a knight in shining armour who agrees to underwrite the liabilities of the lenders within this chain. If a rescuer appears on the horizon, then confidence is restored between these institutions and with us. The lenders will start to lend money again, we will start to save with them and all's well that ends well. (I would say that the stem of blood from the open wound of this financial crisis has been contained—for now—but the wound is far from being healed.)

We might question the past and the offering of complex products that were inherently bad, but the fact remains, we now find ourselves in a position that is the weakest—economically—in our history.

Due to the recent past there is almost certainly a need for tougher regulation for the banking institutions and the manner in which they operate, but should any major bank go under, then confidence is undermined. Once confidence is gone, we stop saving and investing into these banks; we withdraw our savings; the banks then have little money to lend to you and I; they make little to no profit, and they too would go out of business.

The perception, of some, as to how the banking system operates is sometimes hard to get across. Do you recall the Northern Rock crisis. Queues of people around the block, wanting to withdraw their money clamouring for safety. I recall one lady coming out of a branch of this particular institution. In an interview she said, to the reporter something like this:

> I have withdrawn all of my savings, I feel so much better now. What's that you say, what am I going to with the cheque? Well, I am going to leave it on the mantelpiece and I will wait to see what happens.

This is TV gold, pure gold! The lady had completely misunderstood the clearing bank system. She believed that the cheque that she held had an intrinsic value in itself. She believed that her money was now safe. She did not understand that until she presented the cheque to another bank, and it was encashed, her money remained invested with Northern Rock.

This illustration shows how perceptions can be flawed and how a lack of education on the basics of finance are lacking in some. I believe that the media also play upon this and they do not always paint the true picture as to what is happening in the markets as a) they have insufficient air time, and b) because many matters are too complex for most of us (me included) and we have no chance of understanding much of what happens in the major stock markets of the world. But if we cannot understand something, how can we apportion blame so easily and with so much confidence when chatting down the pub about this crisis with our mates?

Just the other day on a major prime time news channel, a report came on about the recent rapid fall in house prices. The reporter regaled this sorry and apparently desperate tale, with words that were something like the following:

> House prices have fallen in the past two months. Last month they fell by 1.3%, this is the highest fall this year; the previous month they fell by 1%; that is a total of a 2.3% fall. People here, in the West Midlands, the worst affected area of the country, are worried. House owners are having to reduce the value of their houses, like the owners of this house behind me. They have had to reduce the price of their house by £7,000, just to get anyone interested. This is a dramatic change as in the first six months of the year house prices rose by 7%.

Now let's examine this statement that was given by a respected national broadcaster. House prices are up by 7% in the year; if you deduct the drop of 2.3% you are left with a net gain of 4.7% in 8 months. This is a fantastic level of growth! As for the reportedly lowest drop in the year; the reporter implied that there have only been two falls in eight months, by a simple process of elimination one of the two falls was bound to be the biggest! (There may have been more drops during the year than this, but the implication of the report was that there had been just the two.) Finally, house owners dropping their asking price by £7,000, this sounds dramatic doesn't it? But how much is the house on the market for? Is this so called dramatic drop in price, a decline of 1%, 3%, 5%? How does the reduction in price relate to the general trend?

This type of reporting is simply ridiculous. It is mere speculation, a distortion of, and a clear manipulation of the facts. But this is the type of reporting that has bombarded our TV screens, radios and newspapers for many years. This type of speculative implied journalism is now rife. It is particularly prevalent in the reporting of the banking crisis.

When considering the banking crisis, we must also acknowledge that many of the issues are more complex than the percentage rise and fall in house prices. For example, do you understand, and can you analyse the nature of: Leveraged Loans? High Yield Bonds? The Special Situations Sector? Corporate Bonds? Government Gilts? Zero Coupons? Split Capital Trusts? The P/E ratio? Short Selling? A Stop Loss Order? The list of job titles that can be attributed to that of a Banker is almost as endless. Understanding who does what is like being an outsider, looking in.

Similarly I could use a collective noun when giving myself a title of being a keen "Angler". I know a lot about rigs; feeders; terminal tackle; spodding; hook patterns; banding baits; the lift method; stret pegging; the knotless knot. The list of equipment and the techniques that I use is almost endless. But, unless you are an "Angler" these terms will be hard to understand. A fellow "Angler" (I enjoy coarse fishing) might still be labelled as an "Angler", but they might practice the art of fishing in a very different manner to myself. For example, the language of a fly fisherman would revolve around: lures; wet fly's; dry fly's; buzzers; leaders; fly patterns etc… There are also sea-anglers who might use beach casting; or perhaps they go wreck fishing offshore. I know little of these other aspects of angling, but we can all be described, collectively, as "Anglers", but we all carry out the art of catching fish in totally different ways.

So it is with Bankers, they all do very different jobs. One set of these so called Bankers may specialise in one sector, or field, of investing, whilst others specialise in another. In reality they may have little understanding of what one another does. To most of us the financial markets are a foreign language and it is all about as understandable (and boring) as me talking about coarse fishing with you! Using the collective noun of *Bankers* as a means of apportioning blame in this economic crisis is, in my opinion, at best misplaced, at worst it is a deliberate scape-goating of a non-existent entity.

I happened to be talking to a city professional the other day, and I mentioned that I was writing this book. I described him as a Banker. Immediately he balked at the notion that anyone could class him as a Banker as in his own eyes he was no such thing. I am yet to find anyone in the city who would describe themselves as a Banker, in the sense that the media uses this title. There are: Discretionary Fund Managers; Investment Managers; Investment Bankers; Merchant Bankers; Brokers of many shapes and sizes etc… There are also many historic titles used in the city that have survived many decades, to make use of this collective noun Banker is, as I say, a misnomer.

I also meet many who are under the mistaken impression that their local high street bank is also stuffed full of wealthy city types who can also be classed as: Bankers. Again, this is simply untrue.

I advocate that continuing to place the blame for the economic mess of today **entirely** at the door of the financial institutions and the Bankers is a case of mistaken identity. After dropping these bombshells, what else can we learn?

As stated, at this time of crisis it is essential to discover who else owns the banks, beside the government. In modern times, the biggest shareholders in the city of London are pension fund managers. If a bank goes under and should the drastic domino effect that I have outlined earlier ever come to pass, should lending facilities dry up, business production and expansion will cease. Companies that have issued shares will either go bust, or survive by ticking along. In this instance all of our own retirement funds are then affected to a potentially devastating degree.

Firstly, all of the guaranteed pension schemes of your local GP; Nurse Practitioner; beat bobby; care worker etc… would probably run into a deficit position, as these schemes would probably be unable to meet their liabilities. What would the government do then? The guarantees of these pension schemes would either have to be dropped, or the state would have to step in and plough huge amounts into pensions funds in order to prop up these schemes and meet their liabilities. (Many of these schemes are in a major deficit position.) What of the many millions of us who are members of private pension schemes? The government is highly unlikely to step in and prop up all of our pension pots, even if they had the money to do so?

We could take up the option of supporting the collective pension pots of state employees through higher rates of taxation. Inevitably this means less money being spent by us in the shops, this results in less profits for business, which means less jobs, resulting in far less revenue in tax being collected by the government from business, we would then see a rise in unemployment, consequently we would see a higher benefit bill for the state and we go full circle as there are more defaults on credit liabilities when we lose our jobs, this means less profits for the lenders, the lenders go out of business etc… I hope that you can see where this is going.

You may find much of this boring and mundane, but before we jump to any conclusion, we need to consider just who we are pointing the finger at. At present we are blaming a collective of people that is too nebulous.

I also believe that, in any such collapse, it is almost inevitable that those at the bottom of the ladder of society will suffer the most.

Therefore I care about all strata of society, rich and poor, for the one affects the other. In history there are both good and bad wealthy and poor people. Christians sometimes forget that Yeshua (Jesus) met with the wealthy tax collectors, as well as meeting with the outcast, the prostitutes and the poor. Yes, his teaching often rebukes those in power, for it is often aimed at the wealthy, but, as I have said and I will continue to repeat, the teaching of this man is not concerned with our wealth, instead he strikes at our hearts. Once our hearts are changed, then our attitude towards our wealth will change. (We will return to this theme time and again in this book.)

A distinct example of Yeshua (Jesus) meeting with the wealthy is that of Zacchaeus. You may recall that Zacchaeus was a tax collector. But he was not just any old tax collector, he was the chief tax collector for the region. He was a top notch government official. You did not want to mess with him. But he wanted to get close to Yeshua (Jesus) as he walked by. Zacchaeus was a short geezer, he couldn't see what was going on, so he shinned up a tree to get a better view. Yeshua (Jesus) saw him, perched up high in a sycamore tree, he called Zacchaeus down from his perch. Yeshua (Jesus) then went to this wealthy man's house to dinner. Over the tea table a dramatic change came about. Zacchaeus had an astounding change of heart. He swore a public oath to give back more than he had taken from all those that he had swindled.

This is just one example of such a transformation, but to me, it is apparent that my arbitrator shows that wealth in itself is not bad. Corruption sits at the door of all of our hearts, waiting for an opportunity to sneak in. It may be a small thing that we do, perhaps we tell an innocent white lie when we file an insurance claim, after all you've paid all those premiums for so many years, why shouldn't you? It's more than you deserve, isn't it? The knock on effect may be pretty minor, but the reality is that for every dodgy insurance claim for a few quid, the premiums of other policy holders are likely to be adversely affected as they will increase in accordance with the number of claims submitted.

Such activity might appear to be a minor offence, in our eyes, but most people start in a small way. I bet your bottom dollar that Zacchaeus started with a small scam of some sort.

Here is a story of another person, in more modern times, who started relatively small. Do you recall Joyti De-Laurey. You may not know the name. She was a Personal Assistant to the mega wealthy employees of the financial institution Goldman Sachs. Here is a summary of her story:

> One Scott Mead was, at the time, an investment banker working within Goldman Sachs. This American financier made his fortune by advising upon and being involved in some of the biggest deals within the booming telecom sector of the late nineteen nineties.
>
> In one particular deal, when advising Vodafone on their £131 billion hostile bid for the German company Mannesman, both he and his employer

earned many millions. (When this Harvard educated Mead retired, aged just 48, his own fortune was estimated to have been in the region of an excess of £100 million.)

Whilst he appears to have been competent at looking after the money of other's, rather embarrassingly he appears to have paid little attention to some of his own financial affairs.

As Mead was wheeling and dealing his lowly secretary Joyti De-Laurey—whose own earnings were reputed to have been in the region of £28,000, excluding annual bonuses and additional tips, which, when they were added to her basic salary, made up a total annual salary package of around £43,000—was able to steal £4.4 million from the private accounts of her bosses, including Mead.

This lowly secretary had previously worked in car sales. Reportedly she joined Goldman Sachs on a salary of £7.50 an hour as a temp in 1998.

She became a permanent employee after demonstrating that she was able to perform at a high level in a very demanding environment. She was prepared to take calls, from her bosses, well into the night and she would often drop everything in order to help them in their work. She soon gained the nickname of Jot. At one point she was allocated the task of organising the 40th birthday party of one her bosses that took place in Italy. It is said that she even acted as toastmaster at the celebratory bash!

One begins to wonder why someone on a basic salary of below £30,000 was prepared to do all of this extra-curricula unpaid work. Shouldn't alarm bells have been ringing earlier and very loudly, in the ears of her bosses?

Jot appears to have become so intoxicated by the enormity of the wealth that she could see around her, she wanted some of the action. She grabbed at the opportunity. The perfect secretary began to take what she wanted.

It seems that she started relatively small as her first act of fraud is reported to have been the forging of one of her bosses signature's, on a cheque, for £4,000. But this was just the hors-d'œuvre! Matters soon began to escalate.

It is alleged that eventually she forged over seventy cheques and helped herself to further funds through false money orders that she faxed to the partners' private investment offices at the HQ of Goldman Sachs in New York. She worked for Mead's for less than a single year, but in this short period, apparently she managed to steal from him a staggering £3.4 million! And on just one solitary transaction she is thought to have netted a cool £2.25 million! Yet still no one, let alone Mead's himself, appears to have noticed that anything was awry.

When the net finally closed in, De-Laurey is reported to have said: I took it because it was easy.

She had spent the proceeds of her crime wildly, buying extravagant gifts of jewellery—mainly to impress her friends. She bought a £750,000 villa in Cyprus, nine homes in Britain, a £140,000 powerboat, numerous luxury holidays, trips to sporting events. At the time of her arrest it was discovered that a deposit had been placed on a £175,000 Aston Martin Vanquish.

On another occasion, in a post arrest interview, she said:
> The people at Goldman Sachs lead lives beyond the dreams of characters in Dallas and Dynasty…One of the policemen called me a Robin Hood—I gave a lot away and my bosses…didn't even notice that I'd taken the money. That's how much they've got.

Something that appears to have started relatively small—although it must be acknowledged that £4,000 is a lot of money to some—grew into major fraud.

There was a knock on effect. Scott Mead was forced to admit, in open court, that he'd had an affair. Jot claimed that she was being paid to keep this affair a secret from Mead's wife and family and the business world.[viii]

Jot's own husband ended up in jail and her mother received a suspended sentence.

[viii] You can read more on this story at:
http://www.guardian.co.uk/theguardian/2005/sep/17/weekend7.weekend

Joyti De-Laurey claimed that both her husband and mother knew nothing of the thefts and they have always declared their innocence. One can only imagine how this might have affected the wider family and friends of Jot and her husband.

What is your own reaction to this whole story? Do you feel that the wealthy bosses deserved what they got because they failed to notice that a secretary, on an annual salary of around £28,000, was on a wild spending spree with their dosh? Do you feel sorry for the rich bosses or for De-Laurey, her husband and her mother? On one occasion Jot is reported to have said:

> I don't want to sound arrogant, I know I committed a crime, but I received over 700 letters of support after I was convicted.

I reckon that every one of those 700 letters represents a fair few thousand of the population who did not write to her. If asked, many would give their tacit approval for what she did. From this statement she apparently knows that she committed a crime, but there appears to be no regret or repentance for this crime.

And what of the mistress of Scott Mead? It has been reported that she has split up from her own husband. But, were children involved in that marital breakdown? Did they suffer at all? Did their school work suffer? What of the friends of De-Laurey? Did they have to relinquish their gifts, as they were proceeds of crime? (I don't know the answer to this legal technicality.)

On such a story as this, the amount of money involved will almost certainly mar our own judgement. If the amount of fraud was say £150, or even a grand, this would never have made the headlines? What if De-Laurey had stopped at £4,000? Would she have ever been found out? I doubt it. But if she had been discovered, then she would probably have been sacked, no more would have been said. The affair of Mead's would never have come to light in open court. It is likely that all of the parties lives would have continued as normal, save for that of a sacked secretary. It is the enormity of the fraud that makes it juicy, almost enjoyable. Many of us become voyeurs, interested in the nitty gritty and we want to know the sordid details. Wealth and opportunity, wow, a heady cocktail.

I was once talking to some investment journalists, about a well known top notch Investment Banker, in a top firm in the city. Apparently he frequently enjoys the company of high class prostitutes. On more than one occasion he had been caught out and he has had to go home grovelling to his wife. None of us are perfect, I am as much a sinner as anyone else, but this is an intelligent man, who is intoxicated by wealth, the earthly power that it brings and the ability to buy naked flesh for a night. Perhaps he gets a buzz from this. Wealth can send the most sensible of men into a spiral of decline and it can severely distort anyone's judgement.

We can, in the case of Jot, see her as one of the good guys, we think good on you. This theory is backed up by the letters of support that she received. But we have, on earth, laws that vary according to severity of the crime. These are epitomised in the Mikado by Gilbert and Sullivan, when the chorus sing:

> His objective all sublime
> He will achieve in time —
> To let the punishment fit the crime —
> The punishment fit the crime;
> And make each prisoner pent
> Unwillingly represent
> A source of innocent merriment!

In the case of Jot and her bosses theft is theft. The amount stolen, no matter how hard it is to swallow, is irrelevant. But to us, as fallen judgemental human beings, the amount means something, it helps us to categorise things. But if it were a plumber from say Poland, and if he was in this country defrauding the state of benefits, now that would be another story all together. Such fraud would cause outrage and letters about immigration control would fly off to the press. Those in power would be lambasted to do something now. But is not theft, theft, whether it be from a rich city boss or through the benefit system?

Perhaps in the case of De-Laurey she was simply intoxicated by the wealth that she could see, touch and almost taste. Was it that tangible? The motivating factor for her actions, appears to have been riches for riches sake. I also wonder if her bosses simply delegated things to her because they could not be bothered. In my book delegation is not spelled: d u m p i n g. Anyone who does so devalues the worth of a co-worker. Perhaps Jot was simply dumped upon and this affected her choices. I don't know, it's just a theory.

My Arbitrator has something to say of Jot, and the city Bankers and institutions. Read Luke, Chapter 16:

> [10]"Whoever can be trusted with very little can also be trusted with much, and whoever is dishonest with very little will also be dishonest with much. [11]So if you have not been trustworthy in handling worldly wealth, who will trust you with true riches?

Jot was trusted, implicitly by her bosses. This trust was clearly misplaced, though this is something that Jot herself would disagree with. The teaching of the Holy Bible is clear that trust has to be there, deeply embedded within all things, and this must mean financial transactions. The question remains: can we now trust these Bankers and institutions or are there still fault lines in the financial markets of the world?

The scriptures, from the outset, highlights how these flaws of mankind come creeping into the created order, with grave consequences. When man and woman have been created they have the whole of creation at their disposal. Despite having access to the totality of God's goodness, they are tempted to turn their back upon all that they have, by considering what is restricted and barred from them:

> [15]The LORD God took the man and put him in the Garden of Eden to work it and take care of it. [16]And the LORD God commanded the man, "You are free to eat from any tree in the garden; [17]but you must not eat from the tree of the knowledge of good and evil, for when you eat of it you will surely die.[ix]

[ix] This can be found in the book of Genesis, Chapter 2, Verses 16 and 17. The account of the temptation of mankind can be found in the same book, Genesis, Chapter 3.

Whether you believe this to be an allegorical or real account, I cite this story to illustrate that the heart of man can be tempted to turn away from what they have, towards that which is denied of them, even when what they have is so very good.

Just like the first man and woman, De-Laurey had the opportunity to help herself to what was barred from her, and she grabbed it, apparently hungrily, with both hands. It is a replaying of the Garden of Eden story.

The bosses at Goldman Sach's—just like Adam and Eve—had wealth beyond imagination. Adam and Eve were given the entire spread of creation, they had it all, they had access to wealth of the highest order, yet they still wanted more. When they had the opportunity, they came wanting to partake and taste what was forbidden from them. The concept of eating and gorging upon the forbidden fruit was appealing, far more exciting than the rest of creation. The wealth of the garden that was before Adam and Eve was for their enjoyment and their pleasure, but also for their sustenance. It had come into being through the bounty and the power of God's creativity. Adam and Eve lost sight and perception of what the created order was for. They lost sight of God. The bosses of Jot at Goldman Sachs, and many other bosses in financial companies throughout the major financial capitals of the world, have lost sight of the true value of money and what wealth is for. They are—and became—so cocooned in the wheeler dealer world of finance, that they lost sight of the intrinsic value of wealth. Despite all of this, I ask, is that reason enough to applaud someone for stealing from them?

It is the attitude held by both Jot and her bosses regarding wealth that should stand out in this story of De-Laurey and her bosses, rather than the amount of money involved. But for most of us, it is the numbers that will be the attractant, rather than the act of theft by one and the apparent arrogance of the others. I believe that this is a distortion of values. The fact that a PA could steal so much and for this act of theft from personal bank accounts to go unnoticed, is simply bewildering, especially when thinking of the amounts involved.

We return to the issue in hand, are the so called Bankers really responsible for the disasters that have swept through the financial markets world wide. If by

Banker we mean those that I refer to earlier, in part yes they are. Like Jot they have had opportunity placed in front of them and for personal material gain they have been willing to take unnecessary risks with some complex and high risk investment strategies. But let me ask this, would you have done the same? A city investor, let's call him John, recently said this to me:

> Many of those who are criticising Bankers are simply jealous. If they had had the same opportunity, they would have done the same.
>
> Do you really think that anyone, if the shoe was on the other foot, wouldn't have done the same thing?
>
> Look at the MPs and their expenses scandal. What about Euro MPs? That is a scandal waiting to break. Then there is the crisis in Greece and the rest of Europe, this is mainly down to corruption. The world is corrupt. Place an opportunity to become rich in front of someone; it is a rare person who will not take it up.

In a sense, John is probably right. I think that part of the reason that such a tirade of vitriol has been levied at Bankers and MPs is verging on jealousy and the simple fact that *I did not have that opportunity*. I wonder if an MP had been a so called Banker, and if a Banker had been an MP would anything have been any different? I very much doubt it.

What if the fictitious benefit fraudster from Poland had been an MP or Banker, would it have been any different? Of course not. This all harks back to the old story of Cain and Abel, in the Holy Bible. The same emotions of jealousy; arrogance; pride and hatred are all live and kicking here and now. We have become jealous of our metaphorical 'brother' in the city. For example, a friend of mine once said this to me:

> If I could get away with screwing the banks, big time, I would do it. I hate them.

A few years later, when the banking crisis was at its peak, and the MPs expenses

scandal hits the news, this same friend says to me:
> Those MPs, I hate them. It's disgusting what they are doing with our money. They are just a bunch of sharks. They are all out for themselves.

The same person, on the one hand he advocates dishonesty for self and he would, if he could, dream up a scheme to defraud the banks, yet in another breath he wants honesty and probity from an MP.

I am also amused by similar double standards of MPs who have criticised the Bankers for greed, and avarice. Some MPs have been most vehement in their criticism of the financial institutions. But, just a few months later, they themselves had been caught red-handed, with their hands literally in the till. Yet both MPs and the financial institutions have maintained that they had done nothing wrong. For example one MP is reported to have said the following, to the auditors of Northern Rock, post crash:
> You have audited and provided comfort letters for the biggest banking disaster in 150 years. The taxpayer has had to lend Northern Rock £29 billion. Don't you think you need to repay your fees?

Perhaps this MP has a point. How could a well known and renowned auditor oversee a large institution and not see that something so major was amiss? But when this same MP had his own expenses investigated the following was allegedly uncovered:
> Between the years 2002 to 2004, this MP is reported to have regularly claimed £1,255 per month in capital repayments and interest, rather than solely for the £700 - £800 on the interest element of the mortgage, as permitted under the rules in force at the time. When this apparent oversight had been noticed by staff in the House of Commons fees office in September 2004, the MP is reported to have said: Why has no one brought this to my attention before?

This particular MP repaid only *some* of his mistaken excess claim immediately, with the remainder of his claim being offset by future expenses. But shouldn't this

MP have applied the standard that he expected of the auditors of Northern Rock? Shouldn't he have repaid the excess claims in full, immediately and not at a later date, through offsetting? Shouldn't the MP have spotted that his claims were not in line with the rules?

I am not an MP, or an auditor, so who am I to judge, but many have leapt in with criticism being levied at the city institutions and MPs in equal measure. But consider this; when looking under the surface of the news headlines I discover that the MP in question was one of the cheapest blokes in parliament, even with the mistaken claim on his mortgage! But being efficient is doesn't sell newspapers, that is not what we want to read or see on our TVs. We want salacious reports as we feast upon scandal. Probity and efficiency is simply not newsworthy.

Yes, someone should have called foul earlier on some of the decisions that the city financiers were taking. The auditors, regulators, even the Bankers (if you wish to label them as this) are all partially to blame, but the Bankers *are not* solely responsible. This current crisis is about opportunity and a general attitude to wealth and ambition. This is a subject that we will examine more closely shortly.

In closing this chapter, I hope that you can see that Bankers are a wide and varied bunch, though city financiers do often lose sight of the real value of money.

The main recurring theme that I have discovered, whilst writing this tome, is the condition of the human heart. Given the opportunity the heart will often lurch violently in one direction or another; either for good, or bad. The human heart is capable of: judging most harshly; jumping to a mistaken conclusion; scape-goating others; and grabbing at an opportunity—even when theft is involved. The human heart, deep within, is fallen, as my arbitrator will say. Our interpretation of what is good and bad can be so easily distorted. This failing is as old as time itself.

Surgery upon this human condition is required, and it is required fast. Perhaps then and only then, will the world be changed.

Are you ready for a Zacchaeus transformation?

CHAPTER THREE

A SOUND BUSINESS PROPOSITION

I have a business proposition for you.

I would like to ask you to invest at least £150 million into my new venture. For this amount of venture capital, you will be appointed to the board of directors. In fact, why not make you chairman?

We will need to appoint a sales manager. For this role you can appoint anyone you like, but you must agree to give them a large bonus when they join our venture. We will also need to offer a contract assuring the sales manager that they have a job for a fixed term of at least five years. If they decide to leave us within the term of their contract, we do not have to pay them a dime. But if we sack them, for any reason, we have to continue paying their salary of around £4 million every year, for the remaining term of the contract, even if they get another job with a rival firm. The sales manager will bring on board his own admin staff on similar unsackable terms.

We will also need to recruit frontline sales staff. We will pay them several million a year, each, no matter how well, or how badly, they perform. But there is some good news. According to their contracts of employment the sales team can only leave our employment during the months of January, July and August each year. This is a good policy. It means that our sales staff cannot just quit our company. On the downside, we cannot recruit any other sales staff from our rivals outside of these three calendar months each year. We will also have it written into the contracts of our sales personnel, if they want to leave our employment, they cannot be approached by our competitors without our permission. There is a negative to this. We cannot approach the sales staff of other employers—to join us—without gaining the permission of their own management team. If we get short of sales staff, don't worry, we will borrow staff from other companies and this is how we will get around any staff shortages.

We will also own two valuable pieces of real estate. We will use these for sales meetings. One area is kept private and it is used to train our sales staff. We can never utilise any of this private land fully, or sell it, as we require exclusive use for a few hours each week. We find that if we train our sales staff for too long they will get tired and their performance will suffer.

On the second piece of ground we will invite our clients to this ground, perhaps 35 or 40 times each year. Clients are only invited when our sales team are working their hardest. At each of these sales conventions we will only use a maximum of 15 of our sales team. The rest of the team we will continue to reward them with high salaries, but they won't have any real function for most of the year, they are just on standby, in case of sickness, accident or injury afflicting any of our mainstream employees.

We will also sell merchandise. This is where it gets interesting. We will sell this for the highest price that we can to our clients. Most goods will be made overseas as we need to manufacture them as cheaply as is possible. Sometimes we don't question too closely where these goods are made, or where the materials come from, because we need to make as much profit as we can from these sales. We will also sell tickets to the clients who attend each sales conference. Sometimes we will fail to sell much more than half of the available seats for each conference.

Our projections on turnover show—even with large volumes of ticket and merchandise sales—it is highly unlikely that we will ever make a large profit. This is because we are paying our sales team and manager such obscene amounts. But, if we do run out of money there is no need to be overly concerned. Should we need to we will just borrow from the banks. They don't seem to care if we can pay back our loans or not! They offer an easy line of credit.

In summary, for your £150 million, you will be buying into a business that will almost certainly have to borrow from the banks. We have little chance of ever repaying these loans; our sales staff are to be paid millions each year for working between 15 – 35 hours average, each week, including the time that we spend training them; the sales manager and his staff cannot be sacked—because if we sack them we have to carry on paying them—even if they get a job with a rival firm, they may end up with us paying their salary and their new employer also paying a separate salary;

we will own the valuable asset of two pieces of real estate, but we cannot build upon it or sell it because we need it for a few hours use each week. What's that? When do you get paid anything? Oh sorry, didn't I mention that? We don't think that you will ever get your money back. We might have to ask you to give us more capital investment in the future, just to stay afloat. What you aren't interested? But why not it's a great deal, surely, isn't it?

I wonder if you recognised what I have just described to you? It is the state of the national sport of England: Football (our cousins across the pond call it: Soccer). Call the sales manager: the manager, or coach; the sales staff: the squad; and you will have then grasped the lunacy that is professional top flight football.

In England the Premier League is often labelled as the top football league in the world, but it is full of teams that are riddled with debt. Surprisingly there is no shortage of investors—many of whom are very successful businessmen. They are prepared to invest millions in these loss making ventures. But why? It is sheer madness.

If you look at the structure of football in the U.K. it does not make any business sense. Furthermore, many believe that there is little chance of any team, apart from four or five, at most, ever winning the Premier League title, though this may be starting to change.

As an example of business debts here are some estimated figures regarding debt for you, back in February 2010, as published by the Independent:

Manchester United topped the debt ladder with a reported debt of £716 million!

Arsenal came next with a reported £297 million;

Liverpool—who are being ravaged by the owners in-fighting—owed around £261 million (and now they appear to have been rescued by yet another wealthy owner, or a consortium of owners who promise to wipe out the debt);

Fulham owed £164 million;

West Ham owed a paltry estimate of £114 million;

Aston Villa owed £72 million;

Portsmouth, only owed around £57 million;

The other clubs owed varying amounts from around £58 million downwards;

Two clubs, Chelsea and Manchester City have had their substantial debts effectively written off by their very wealthy owners.

Little old Burnley had little debt outside of the directors of the board of the club.[ix]

Will any of these clubs ever be debt free. Consider what has happened to some of these clubs at the end of the 2009/2010 season.

Manchester United, finished second in the title race, and lifted no meaningful silverware.

Chelsea won the Premier league title along with the oldest cup competition in the world, the F.A. Cup.

At the other end of the scale, Portsmouth almost went into administration and went to court to battle with the taxman over unpaid taxes. They now face second tier football. Many were surprised when the judge allowed Portsmouth to continue, when any other business would almost certainly have been shut down over unpaid taxes.

Apparently it is fine for a football club to avoid paying tax, but for Bankers to be paid a bonus, upon which they pay tax, this is often considered to be an outrage!

Although little old Burnley had little or no debt, they were relegated.

All of this reveals something obvious. Without a significant injection of money, and some form of multi-million pound backing from a sugar daddy, Malay businessman, Russian oligarch, or oil sheikh, a football team has absolutely no chance of winning the Premier League title. Even survival in the top flight depends upon debt and some form of multi-millionaire backing a club.

[ix] Please read more on football debt at: http://www.independent.co.uk/sport/football/premier-league/the-debt-league-how-much-do-clubs-owe-1912244.html

This leads me to another question: why does any successful businessman (or woman) wish to invest into an enterprise based upon the current ludicrous structure of a club accruing large debts, with ever increasing bank loans and a potentially nil rate of return?

I also wonder why the banks ever lend money to these so called businesses? Any other business that is set up under such a system would have no chance of gaining such enormous lines of credit, especially in the current economic climate?

Why have I looked at football in a book about the banking crisis and the so called credit crunch? Let's examine matters a little further.

We might accept the ludicrous nature of something such as football—insert your own sporting passion—and due to our passionate involvement as a supporter we may turn a blind eye to the excesses involved in sport—and even wider than this, we seem to accept the affluence of a whole raft of sporting stars such as: football players, F1 drivers, tennis players, golfers, and such like—but when we see Bankers being awarded bonuses, we become riled. Why? (My dad used to call football 22 idiots kicking a bag of wind! In a sense he was right. In the context of the problems that are facing the world, football is pretty insignificant.)

We currently live in a society where we have been quick to blame Bankers for irresponsible lending decisions, but when considering our own passions, such as football, all of our own rationale also goes out of the window. We do not appear to be that bothered about the ***ludicrous lending criteria that the banks might employ*** when they are deciding whether to advance large loans to the football club that we support.

It is a similar situation with salaries. Bankers, if they are recipients of massive bonuses, this is considered to be immoral. They have got us into the current mess that we face. But what of football icons. They sign up to contracts that are clearly unaffordable in the longer term. These contracts could cause the club that we support, with a passion, to go bust? On the one hand we can be derogatory of Bankers, but of our sporting icons, the most we might do is shrug our shoulders at the large levels of pay that they receive. It is fine for soccer players to be paid a salary equivalent to that of a Banker and to be able to spend it all on the so called "high life". For many supporters the morals of their star players are not even considered to be on the radar of morality. We might be concerned about the latest signing to our club and whether they can score twenty plus goals in a season, for this is what matters most to us. For a Banker to be paid according to their performance, this is highly objectionable. (I am also intrigued that when Bankers spend their bonuses in a casino or bar, this is something that is to be scorned. How dare they spend our money in such a lavish manner. But an England striker smoking and urinating in a street, paying for prostitutes, all of this is shrugged off as just being high jinx or something that he will learn from, especially when reprimanded by his club manager! Don't get me onto the manner in which supporters, managers and players treat match officials. This behaviour defies all rationale.)

Of course there is a huge difference between a Banker and a footballer. The actions of the one affects most of us quite markedly, in financial terms, whereas the salary of a football player does not affect our material wealth directly. For the recipients of these massive salaries and bonuses, whether they be a footballer or a Banker, I would imagine that the motivating factor is exactly the same. Fortunes are on offer, so why not take it?

But, when things go wrong, our fallen nature becomes evident as our sinful nature rises up within us. We want to pin the blame upon someone. If our team is fighting relegation, then it has to be someone's fault, whether this be the manager; the players; the board; or the wealthy owners and their in-fighting that has ruined our club. We might shout and swear at any of the above; perhaps some fans will hold protest marches; or at the start of a match the supporters will turn their back on the board, chanting against the subject of their ire; or they may stand there, in silence.

When it comes to the economy, we have fallen into the same trap. We have to blame someone for the financial crisis. This propensity to blame others appears to be inherent within our character. It crosses the boundaries of leisure and is firmly embedded in the reality of life.

In the past we have been able to vent our frustration on politicians, with some just cause. The Chancellor of the Exchequer runs the economy, perhaps it is their policies that got us into this mess; or it is the Prime Minister, after all he led us into an illegal war, or two.

But now the blame game has gone full circle. The politicians have discovered an alternative whipping boy to blame, which has enabled them to shift the target from themselves, to the Bankers. Clearly, they say, it is not the fault of any economic or foreign policy of parliament, it is the greedy Bankers that are to blame.

But, in politics too, there have been so many revelations of abject greed. The expenses scandal in the U.K. that hit the press in 2009 took the media by storm. The common defence of politicians was the simple mantra: We did not break the rules!

Across society, when jobs are under threat or if our football team is not doing well, if MPs are found out to be more corrupt than we first imagined, we want to apportion blame. Nothing is ever our fault. We can be extremely judgemental beings. The media is generally happy to stoke up these feelings of indignation, whether our target be Bankers, politicians or footballers, as this sells newspapers.

Football is perhaps a reflection of our wider so called civilised society. In the last twenty years or so it has, and it continues to live, in a world of excess where the few are rewarded at the expense of the majority. Great fortunes can be accumulated by individuals not really doing a great deal apart from knocking a sphere of inflated leather around a field. It really is not that important! The news headline is stark though. Both football and society are now living well beyond their means. At some point a crisis point will be arrived at in both scenarios. The national sport of England is bust as a viable business model (not that it ever was that viable). The excesses within this sport (and in many others) are simply unsustainable. There is a finite resource bank out there and when multi-millionaire businessmen wake up they will stop investing and the banks will stop lending. Financial collapse of football—and many other sports—is simply inevitable, at some point a large club will disappear and go bust.

The wider question for our economy, as with football, is whether the economies of the world can be rescued, or is it too late? Are they, like football, also bust?

Just like football, in banking the extremes of affluence for the few, is also questionable. But again, as with football, when our "team" (i.e. our pension funds and ISAs) were winning all was well. The economy was hunky-dory and few complained of the "players" (i.e. the city financiers) receiving high levels of salary and bonuses.

We appear to have, within us, an ability to pass harsh judgement upon others, in many rafts of society, if the worst should happen.

As I have said, my arbitrator has so much to say about these judgemental tendencies and how we should view one another. I love one example in the Holy Bible that shows how we should treat one another. Rather than viewing one another with judgement and condemnation, Yeshua (Jesus) shows us a rather different way. A woman is caught in the act of committing adultery—this means that she was almost certainly a prostitute. At the time, the penalty for this sinful act was death by stoning. But, Yeshua (Jesus) steps in and says this to the crowd that is baying for her blood:

> If any one of you is without sin, let him be the first to throw a stone at her.

Yeshua (Jesus) was (according to the Holy Bible) perfect. Therefore the underlying sub text for us today is:

> If you dare to do so; throw a stone, but beware, I am perfect and I am not going to stone her; dare you still throw that stone in your hand? If you are untainted by sin and immorality, then you have my permission to proceed with this stoning.

Before we cast the first stone at anyone—whether our aim be at footballers; football team managers; board room directors; let alone the Bankers, we need to turn our focus away from the amount of money involved, no matter how unpalatable this is and view one another as the ultimate of God's creation and that we are all the same fallen beings, as no one is perfect.

In the consumerist society that we live in, wealth and judgementalism has come to rule our desires and our hearts. We are within a cycle of jealousy, vitriol and self interest. In the financial cities of the world this has led to a need for greed itself. Greed became the new "red". It was (and still appears to be) trendy and chic to watch Top Gear and drool after the fast super cars. It became cool to have a lifestyle that meant bigger homes, better holidays and more stuff. And if you could not afford it, do not worry, put it on the plastic, take out a loan, pay it back some time in the future.

At some point though, someone should have put the brakes on these lines of credit. Whether this should have been the government; the regulator of the lending institutions; or through voluntary self-regulation; at some point, someone somewhere should have said:

> Stop, halt! You want to borrow how much? You want to have how much on your credit card? No way, you will have to save up for it. You cannot have it now, you may want it now, but you can't because it is simply too risky!

But, as our sporting, film and pop icons got richer, and as the city got richer, the rest of us (or at least the majority of us) wanted to emulate the wealth that we read about and the lifestyles that we saw on our TVs each and every day.

So yes, the lending institutions are guilty, they should have stopped lending so much, so easily. They should have said:

> If you want a house, then we will individually assess your ability to pay the mortgage. Let's look at your track record and examine things. What's your long term employment been; how about the future?

Instead, when lending money to us, the lenders looked at narrow snapshots of our lives, over brief periods of time. Upon the basis of this narrow corridor of our lives, lenders decided to lend and lending boomed. If you wanted to borrow money, it did not appear to matter if you had been bankrupt; or how many County Court Judgements (CCJs) were against your name. Many banks simply lent money, with little regard to the future and the ability of borrowers to repay the loans that they granted, in the longer term.

But are the lenders solely to blame? Weren't they simply feeding the need and the hunger of their clients? I believe that we need to consider things far more carefully than the media portrays. I will discuss the whole arena of lending policies in more detail shortly.

What we do need to consider is what stones we are about to pick up and throw, before opening our mouths and condemning people, even Bankers, out of hand. This is a lesson that I myself still struggle with. The Bible has much to say about reining in our speech. In the Book of James and Chapter 3, it says:

> [1]Not many of you should presume to be teachers, my brothers, because you know that we who teach will be judged more strictly. [2]We all stumble in many ways. If anyone is never at fault in what he says, he is a perfect man, able to keep his whole body in check.
>
> [3]When we put bits into the mouths of horses to make them obey us, we can turn the whole animal. [4]Or take ships as an example. Although they are so large and are driven by strong winds, they are steered by a very small rudder wherever the pilot wants to go. [5]Likewise the tongue is a small part of the body, but it makes great boasts. Consider what a great forest is set on fire by a small spark. [6]The tongue also is a fire, a world of evil among the parts of the body. It corrupts the whole person, sets the whole course of his life on fire, and is itself set on fire by hell.
>
> [7]All kinds of animals, birds, reptiles and creatures of the sea are being tamed and have been tamed by man, [8]but no man can tame the tongue. It is a restless evil, full of deadly poison.
>
> [9]With the tongue we praise our Lord and Father, and with it we curse men, who have been made in God's likeness. [10]Out of the same mouth come praise and cursing. My brothers, this should not be. [11]Can both fresh water and salt water flow from the same spring? [12]My brothers, can a fig tree bear olives, or a grapevine bear figs? Neither can a salt spring produce fresh water.

No man can tame the tongue, wow! The words that can so very easily trip off the tongue can cause wars; inspire crowds to hate others—whether this be on the terraces or on the battlefield, or in the media when referring to Bankers. But if we spew out hatred, it is just a reflection of what lies within our hearts. Self control is something to learn, a discipline that we need to be willing to take on board. We can curse our fellow man (or woman), and we can easily fall into the trap of holding icons and celebrities in contempt, poking fun at them in quite a hurtful manner. This same behaviour can extend to Bankers. The tongue, can corrupt the whole person! These are also strong words that carry a dire warning. I think—because the tongue is a reflection of what is within the heart—if we stop for a moment to take the time to consider our words carefully, inwardly our hearts will become transformed. When the heart has undergone this self inflicted surgery then perhaps the media reports on the Bankers and the banking crisis would be less condemning and far less misleading. But many of us find this form of discipline unpalatable.

I realise that the concept of processing words from our mouths is a long way from the opening of this chapter, but I am trying to show that our passions and emotions can be contradictory. On the one hand we hold Bankers who earn fortunes in contempt, but our heroes, within our celebrity obsessed culture are granted a great deal of latitude and tolerance. We want our sporting clubs to do well at all costs, we can accept the utter stupidity of the lending policies of the banks in order to fund the excessive—and some would say obscene—payrolls of our sporting heroes, but on the other hand we condemn the lending policies of the banks when they allegedly cause a break down of the economy due to the very same bad lending policies. This is contradictory. I am not laying the blame for the economic crisis at the door of sport, but I hope that you can see we can be passionate, irrational beings. At times we are ready to use our voices to hurt, or to heal, or encourage. Emotions, desires and loyalty are not wrong in themselves, but we need to constantly evaluate what is important and take care not to use inflammatory language and condemnation when speaking of others—including the Bankers.

The Holy Bible is clear that each of us has individual responsibility. There are also consequences to actions, we know this. We do not have to read the Holy Bible to understand this, but, in this current crisis we must move away from a blame culture; a culture that lays the problems of today at the door of one solitary profession and a small group of individuals will not solve anything. Such a levelling of blame may make us feel better for a while, but it achieves little else.

I believe that the media need to report news yes, but creating an environment of blame with a rhetoric and language that is quite damning at times, does not solve anything. Some of the language used in the reports upon this crisis is, at times I feel, misplaced and—as I have tried to show—inaccurate. There is a need to tame the tongue somewhat. I agree that the lending policies of the financial institutions were irrational and irresponsible, but so was the response of the many of us who took up the option to borrow when they could, without giving much thought or regard to the future.

This leads me nicely onto the next topic, where I need to tread very carefully indeed.

CHAPTER FOUR

NEITHER A BORROWER NOR A LENDER BE

Let's kick off this chapter with a famous quotation.

> Neither a borrower nor a lender be;
> For loan oft loses both itself and friend,
> And borrowing dulls the edge of husbandry.

This is a quotation from the play, Hamlet, by William Shakespeare. It is the advice that a father, Polonius, gives to his son Laertes before the young man leaves for pastures new. In the context of the play Polonius is eventually exposed as a foolish prattling knave. In some productions of the play he is played as a buffoon; in others he is portrayed as being senile and deranged. Perhaps there is more truth in the ramblings of this old man than one might think.

The advice given is simple; don't lend to, or borrow from, friends. If you lend to a friend then the loan might be forever lost as the borrower may not be able to repay the debt; furthermore you may lose a friendship over the resulting unpaid liability. The last line advises that if, as a borrower, you have easy access to a line of credit this can reduce the intrinsic value of savings, possessions, or anything that you own as you may fail to be a good steward.

Though these words were penned many hundreds of years ago, there is much truth in them, as we are beginning to discover. For many years the West has maintained an easy line of credit, both personally, and as a corporate society. But how did this line of credit for the nation begin? Here is a short potted history:

> Prior to late into the 17th century, the state would fund the cost of going to war by levying new and often higher taxes. In 1694 the Nine Years War left the English Government virtually bankrupt. The government of the time borrowed £1.2 million, at a rate of 8%, from the newly formed Bank of England. The result was the birth of national deficit financing, or the National Debt.

The more modern National Debt emerged in the early 18th century and the amount of that government debt rose from £1.2 million at the start of the 18th century to £850 million by the end of the Napoleonic Wars in 1815.

Another major increase of the country's debt occurred during World War One, when it increased from £650 million in 1914, to a significantly higher amount of £7.4 billion in 1919.

The second world war saw another major increase. By the end of the second world conflict in 1946, the National Debt of the U.K. had grown to £24.7 billion.

The level of National Debt has been through various phases of increasing and decreasing, since. Historically Britain has maintained a good credit worthy status in the world's eyes. This solid and dependable status is now seriously under threat.

More recently however it is a very different story, which is disturbing many economists. In the U.K. (and the picture is very similar across many nations) the level and the manner of debt has taken a more worrying turn. It can be said that the U.K. is accruing (or has already accrued) a National Debt that is the amount that it would require to fight a global conflict. This is extremely worrying. Currently, every year in the U.K. the Government spends more money than it raises in taxation, by a long, long way.

In order to plug the gaping hole of overspend the government offers a seemingly simple solution. You lend me some money and we will give to you a guaranteed return of your capital with interest. They issue what are known as Government Bonds. These investments are collectively known as gilts. Once the government has secured a loan they spend the money but on, or by, a fixed date in the future all of these gilts have to be repaid in full with interest. The total value of all of these loans (and a few others) currently makes up the National Debt. The people who invest in or buy gilts are mainly institutional investors, both in the U.K. and overseas (you and I can buy some gilts if we so wish—you may have heard of National Savings, these are also a form of government debt). By institutions I mean pension and investment fund managers. Once again, within the financial markets there is an intrinsic link to your retirement nest egg.

Over the past few years the National Debt has grown quite considerably. In order to gain a handle on this burden here are some basic figures. Since 1976 the U.K. has been running an ever increasing budget deficit. This means that the government sold more gilts and bonds than it repaid. It continued to sell more and more debt every year that passed by in order to raise enough money to run the country in the manner that they saw fit.

The government did not borrow this money to buy property, like you or I might, instead it borrowed money to pay for essential items. For example, currently the biggest cost to the government is the welfare state. It is estimated that this bill will shortly amount to around £202.6 billion, or more! The welfare budget includes expenditure on:

> state pensions;
> tax credits;
> unemployment benefits;
> sickness benefits;
> housing benefits;
> child support payments;
> with a whole raft of other benefits.

Another worrying trend is that the cost of the National Debt—in the U.K.—has risen in 2010, to a level whereby the interest payments alone amount to just less than the entire education budget for the nation. This means that the bare essentials of what we have come to expect as a right, such as free health care, education, law enforcement and state benefits is all becoming more and more unaffordable as things stand. (The students are now taking to the streets over future increases in fees. This is all very honourable, but just taking to the streets is rather pointless I feel, unless they have an alternative. One student leader on national radio likened their struggle to that of Martin Luther King! Hmm. This student really needs to re-read history one feels, or at least ensure that they only offer non-destructive peaceful demonstrations.)

A result of this rapidly accumulating figure is that the National Debt has increased to such a level that the U.K. government is now paying interest in the region of £43 - £44 billion during this current year alone!

It is worth pointing out that in itself debt may not be unhealthy, many of us have a mortgage, which is a form of debt, we borrow money in order to buy a house to live in, but prior to taking out a loan you are assessed by a lender as to whether you can afford to repay a loan (as I have said these assessments have acquired too narrow a range of data—until now). With the government I wonder who is conducting a real in depth assessment upon the ability of the U.K. government to repay their debts? Debt becomes unhealthy when the interest payments, or the debt cannot be repaid on time. This is where the country sits right now, the debts are mounting and the chances of the government ever paying it back in full is diminishing, unless radical action is taken. Do you recall the example of football in the previous chapter? The country finances are going in the same direction as soccer, directly south, and very rapidly.

In 2009-2010, the Government spent, give or take a few pounds, £671.4 billion. The income gained in tax receipts—over the same period—have fallen short of this figure by a large margin, they are only around £496.1 billion. ***This means that the government overspend, during the year, was a staggering £175.3 billion!*** I wonder if you can imagine asking your bank for a loan of this magnitude because you have spent more than your annual level of income. Imagine a conversation such as follows:

You: Mr. Bank Manager.

Bank Manager: Yes.

You: Er I'm a bit short of cash this month.

Bank Manager: Yes.

You: Can I borrow some extra until things turn out a bit better.

Bank Manager: How much do you need?

You: Just £175.3 million please.

Bank Manager: And what do you offer as collateral?

You: Look you know me, we go back to school. Do you remember that time…

Bank Manager: Are you wasting my time?

You: Well er… no, not really.

Bank Manager: So what security do you have.

You: Just that my word is my bond.

Bank Manager: Are you pulling my leg.

You: Er no…

Bank Manager: Is this some kind of joke.

You: I'm prepared to sign a piece of paper saying I will repay you.

Bank Manager: Next.

Your bank is hardly going to say that's fine we trust you, after all we know where you live. But this is how the finances of this country—and many others throughout the world—are being run. Just like the football clubs there is this vague hope that things will get better and one day the debt will be under control.

During 2010-2011 the interest payments on **the National Debt is estimated to be the fourth biggest cost in budget expenditure of this country**. This means that the government is having to borrow an ever increasing amount of money in order to finance the National Debt. This cycle that has no real end point, unless tough action is undertaken. It is a bit like the familiar story of having a credit card that becomes unaffordable. You spend using up your permissible level of credit; at the end of the month you cannot repay what you owe. Eventually, after a few months, you move the outstanding balance to a new credit card. The new company charges you no interest on your balance transfer but you cannot afford to make a payment toward the balance. A couple of months later, when struggling, you take out a personal loan to pay off the credit card company. (For some people they may start to use a brainless company that is currently advertising on the mainstream media.

They lend you money until your pay day, just to make ends meet. Borrowing £50.00 costs a few quid more. But look at the Annual Percentage Interest Rate on these short term loans. It is—incredibly—currently well in excess of 2,000%! To me this is utterly perverse and immoral. In my view the government should introduce legislation that bans such companies out of existence. I believe in a free market economy, but this is simply preying upon the vulnerable. It may be within the rules, but it is shatteringly corrupt lending. Companies such as this are nothing short of loan sharks.) Eventually you might increase the amount of your mortgage in order to repay the loan and credit cards, but the cycle continues. Before long you find yourself in debt again. This has no termination point as you have borrowed money in order to try and keep your head above water to repay your existing debts. Often repossession of your property follows, especially if you suffer illness and you are unable to earn money to meet your debt obligations.

So it is with the manner in which the governments of the past have borrowed money—rather irresponsibly in my view, as they should have known better. (By the way, ALL political parties have been as bad as one another, this practice has been carried out for aeons.)

The other bad news for this absurd policy of the U.K. government is that in order to repay this mounting debt, more and more of the national budget is eaten up solely by interest payments. The net result is that there is far less money to spend on the essential items of education; health; law enforcement; roads; defence etc… Who loses the most? The poorest in society, those on benefits, and those of us who really do rely upon the likes of the NHS and the state education system and other welfare provision.

Another worry is that all governments continue to assume that investors will continue to buy gilts in order to fund this ever increasing level of expenditure. Investors appear to be happy to rely upon the guarantees of the British government, but, if investors get twitchy and if their confidence falls they will move away from investing into gilts. As a consequence, the demand for gilts can fall and the value of gilts can decline. The net result is that some gilts will cost less to buy, the yield (or returns) can then start to rise on these gilts resulting in a higher level of interest payments for every penny borrowed by the government. For you and me, this means higher mortgage interest rates.[x]

This situation is not unique to the finances of the U.K. as many Western economies are in the same boat. This continuing level of spiralling debt must have a consequence and an end point. The question is, what will that final outcome be?

So that is the national outlook. The economy of the U.K.—and the economy of many Western countries—is simply shot to pieces. Depending upon your political leanings you may believe that one route or the other is the answer.

It has also just been announced that European countries are going to lend to Ireland billions to bail out the Irish economy. Is this necessary? On paper it is. The U.K. exports more to Ireland than several developing countries combined, but I still wonder about this lending policy. We have borrowed so much as a nation that we are struggling to pay back the National Debt. A raft of cuts are now being proposed and will bite shortly, and yet we are now lending to another nation vast amounts of money!

The concept of a global economy structured in the way it is currently, is a broken concept. It is unhealthy to have banks, and institutions, so big and international that we cannot allow them to fail. It is also unhealthy to have countries that are so inter-dependent upon one another that we feel compelled to bail them out, for if we do not they will go to the wall and bring us down with them. In contrast I struggle with walking away from the concept of being my brother's keeper. If we have the money to ensure that poverty does not strike, then perhaps we should use the wealth of the country to shore up the broken economies of others. In reality no one knows what to do. Most are agreed that the current structure needs fixing, but no one really knows how to do it. It is like manning the pumps on a doomed ship. You can only pump out so much of the water that is flooding in for so long, you can whack bungs into the hole of the hull, but unless you get into port and safe harbour quickly the

---

[x] Please read more on gilts at:
http://www.moneywise.co.uk/grow-money/investing/article/2010/04/13/are-gilts-really-safe-bet

ship **will** sink. In this scenario the survivors will be left in life rafts and amongst the wreckage hoping against hope for rescue. The longer that it takes for rescue to take place then tempers in the lifeboats will fray. Factions will form. Eventually bitter rivalry will rise up and war will break out between those in the life boat, who now guard jealously what is theirs refusing to trade their rations with one another. They will point accusing fingers at others of a different mind-set.

In reality we have lost the Biblical principle of two things. The honour of the borrower to repay the debt, and the fairness of the lender to forgive the debt at specific intervals. This principle of trust and fairness is gone, as has the concept of not charging interest upon a loan by the lender. But more on this a little later.

The truth is, until now, mankind has always believed that big is beautiful and a global fast moving economy with domination by the few is good. I would argue that big is anything but beautiful and that this global economy being dictated to by a few large firms is unhealthy and uncontrollable.

It is against this difficult political and financial background that I often see many friends on social networking sites badgering politicians to resolve complex social justice issues. Often these same issues are tied up in the complexities of the economy. Though these requests may be well meaning, I do not believe that politicians can do very much on many matters. Yes they can promise the earth, but they will seldom be able to deliver.

As an aside I liked the slogan of a politician's recent election campaign—in the Philippines I think—as it was refreshing and remarkably truthful:

I'll do my best, but, I can't promise anything.

Currently politicians have some extremely difficult decisions to make. Do they raise taxes? Should they cut spending? Whatever they do, someone, somewhere, will lose out and their actions will appear to be unjust. Furthermore, it takes between three to seven years for economic decisions to filter through. We all want action, and we want it now in our satisfy me now type of society—and we have evolved into a give it to me now so that I can gain immediate gratification culture—we also want to see better health care, education, more police on the streets, all with immediate effect. Many of us also want to see the bonuses of Bankers to be curbed and the Bankers to be held to account.

In amongst this pot of mixed emotions I have become evermore dismayed at the lack of leadership of our politicians. The yah-boo politics of our country during this current crisis is futile and, quite frankly, childish. The principles of: I am in government so I must shout you down and you are in opposition so you must oppose everything I say, must surely be abandoned for the sake of the country's welfare and for all of our sakes?

Surely a wider coalition that includes parties of political shades is what is required. Personally I am delighted that at the time of writing, the current U.K. government is consulting a Labour politician on the reform of the welfare state. Frank Field has been calling for change and modernisation of the benefits system for many years.[xi] Irrelevant of his party allegiance, he has been bought into a right of centre government as an adviser. Whether he is right or wrong in his views only time will tell. In principle there is no other politician who knows this subject as well as he does so he should be given a voice at this time of crisis when money needs to go to the poorest and the most vulnerable as quickly and as efficiently as possible. During this time of crisis other politicians need to start acting and voting according to their individual conscience rather than along their own enforced party lines. If this means a compromise of electioneering manifestos and promises, then so be it. Be the bigger person.

The government, with the media, have been very quick to blame Bankers for the current crisis, but due to their own irresponsible borrowing policies, the politicians of the past have been engaged in a policy of tax, borrow and spend, spend, spend. Taking all of the above into account I do not believe that anyone can say for sure what the welfare state will look like in a few years time.

The current level of public spending is unrealistic. We have to face up to the

---

[xi] Please read more in an article by Frank Field at: http://www.telegraph.co.uk/news/newstopics/politics/conservative/7803983/Poverty-is-about-much-more-than-money.html

fact that politicians are required to make some really tough decisions. We have a whacking bill to pay and we have a limited number of stark choices.

1. We can either go on a shopping spree and pay more as we shop, thereby giving the country's coffers more in the way of indirect taxes such as VAT.
2. We can pay far more tax on our earnings and savings.
3. We can give more by making voluntary contributions to the charitable sector, enabling these charities to pick up where the state leaves off.
4. We can get used to the idea—and the reality—of reduced benefits, expenditure and a vastly reduced welfare state.

We are also facing an unprecedented fact. The so called baby boomer generation that were born between 1946 and 1964 are now edging toward retirement. Over the next few years the retired population is going to increase significantly. To expect the younger generation to support the income and health care needs of this group of the retiring populace is a burden that is unsustainable. Time has run out. Successive governments have failed to act, and act swiftly. Tinkering with pensions law throughout the 70s, 80s and 90s is all too little far too late.

Without further immediate radical action the National Debt will continue to mount until it arrives at critical mass, and then…? The best that I can do is to point to the lyrics of a song, by the group ABC:

> I've seen the future,
> I can't afford it,
> Tell me the truth sir
> Someone just bought it
> Say Mr. whispers!
> Here come the click of dice
> Roulette and blackjacks—gonna build us a paradise
> Larger than life and twice as ugly
> If we have to live there, you'll have to drug me…

The problem with these lyrics is that the drugs will also be unaffordable on the NHS!

As with blame for this crisis being apportioned solely to the Bankers, it is also easy to blame politicians for the state of the economy, and yes, they are to blame in part. I hope that I have demonstrated that successive governments have been content to spend without looking to the future. Politicians have failed to address the demographic time bomb of us living longer but still getting sick.

We need to look to ourselves, as much as the Bankers. Most of us don't want to pay higher taxes, whether we be middle class, extremely rich or when we are on the minimum wage. This is why politicians get away with what they do. Thomas Jefferson is credited with saying:

> The government you elect is the government you deserve.

The American journalist, H.L. Mencken, expanded upon this when he said:

> People deserve the government they get, and they deserve to get it good and hard.

I think that this is true. But, we cannot abandon the concept of maintaining a benefit and welfare system, no matter how broke we might be as a nation. Having some form of benefit system is entirely in line with Biblical theology. Caring for the sick, the poor and the dispossessed is, as I hope I have demonstrated to you, close to the heart of the God that I believe in. Social care should be a top priority. But we have grown used to believing that what we have in the way of free health care; education etc… is a right, rather than a privilege. I find it interesting that in our society we often hear the phrase: Human Rights. In the main we generally agree wholeheartedly with maintaining our rights, until someone else's rights contradict our own. We might say:

> We agree with free health care, but only for those who are born here. These immigrants, they have no right to health care, they are jumping the queue and this affects my own access to free health care, what have they ever done for us?

There is insufficient time and space to look at this in detail here, but it is this intrinsic and pervasive self-centred nature that cuts across our perception of wealth that is a recurrent theme in this book.

Once something is labelled as being ours by right it tends to become something that we value far less. Once individuals in society are forced into contributing towards a welfare system, we become embroiled in the argument that we own this nebulous entity that we have paid into. Therefore we have every right to get something back from it, if we don't get what's ours then we will voice our discontent. We might even take to the streets. On occasion we may be prepared to commit violence to gain what we see as a right. The Biblical concept of the farmer leaving a surplus for the poor, is a request made by God, initially. This indicates that this is something that God wants us to do voluntarily. Ideally maintaining a benefit system should be one that comes from the willingness of our hearts.

It has been said, more than once, that the bad lending policy of the banks is **the** reason for the economic mess of today. I agree to an extent that the financial institutions **must** carry some of the can so let's examine the whole issue of lending irresponsibly in a little more detail. Let's kick off with a couple of real life cases, that I have come across in my day to day job as an Independent Financial Adviser (IFA). I have changed the names of my clients in order to protect their identity, but these are real case scenarios. This is case one:

>A married couple, Mr. and Mrs. Tanadi come to me for some advice. Mr. Tanadi was serving as a Gurkha. He'd left the armed forces about three years previously. He now had a main job, and picked up other part time work. He was working hard to get together a deposit for the purchase of a flat.
>
>Since leaving the Gurkha's they had both managed to get together around £30,000 for a deposit. They were currently living in a one bedroom flat, which they were renting at a cost of around £1,200 a month.
>
>They had found a flat, in a fairly decent part of the town. The cost of a mortgage on this property was going to cost them around £800 each month.
>
>To secure a mortgage they would need to borrow close to six times Mr.

Tanadi's income.

Would you lend them the money? Let me tell you a little more.

When examining the bank accounts of this couple they had a surplus in their bank account of between £500 to £900 every month, for the past two years or so. This meant that they were living well within their means.

I found a lender who took a common sense approach and we arranged the mortgage with no issue at all.

This type of lending, that is based upon a multiplying of income has been much criticised in the media. But why? When it is used in this legitimate manner based upon a track record of affordability, it is a valid loan. The income is there on payslips, the deposit is saved up, and there is determination on the part of the couple to make things work. The lender assessed the risk, they looked at the long term history of the clients at management level, in a local branch, and the managers decided to lend the money.

Let me tell you another story. This is case two:

Mr. and Mrs. Hughes wish to carry out some home improvements. They also wished to buy a car for their expanding family. Both Mr. and Mrs. Hughes are working and they hold reasonably secure jobs. In order to gain a mortgage they need to borrow around 110% of the current property value. I arranged the loan for them at just over 110% of the property value.

Would you have leant them the money? This type of lending—in particular the lending criteria of Northern Rock has been lambasted. Let's cut through the headlines and examine this. Mr. and Mrs. Hughes had three choices.

1. Keep the mortgage as it was, and take out a personal loan. These loans would be on quite a high variable interest rate—as no security would be offered to the lender—increasing the combined repayments of a mortgage and a personal loan quite significantly, which would have continued for a

period of perhaps five years.
2. Arrange a loan with Northern Rock who offered a mortgage up to around 85% of the property value combined with an additional personal loan that would be secured against the property for the remaining lending. All at a low interest rate, offering their home as collateral, rather than having a separate personal loan as outlined in option one above.
3. Forget buying a car and the home improvements, thereby negating the need for the additional borrowing.

I wonder which option you would have chosen if you were Mr. and Mrs. Hughes? In the end we elected to arrange borrowing based upon the second option, with around 85% of the property value as a mortgage and a secured personal loan, bringing the total level of borrowing to around 110% of the property value.

There are many peripheral arguments about the personal loan being tied in with the mortgage over a longer term, but my clients ended up with affordable repayments; a car that suited their needs; with a home that could house them, as a family, comfortably.

Despite the media claims of irresponsible lending being levied at Northern Rock, used properly, the concept of their products was a fairly sound proposition. They enabled clients to secure surplus borrowing, in the form of a secured loan, assuming an increase of house values over the longer term, at a far lower interest rate than an ordinary personal loan from a high street lender. The media latched onto a lender offering a mortgage of more than 100% of the property value as being irresponsible. This was not always the case.

The inherent desire to own one's own home has also increased in the West and this drove lending demand of the banks, by the society at large, upwards. In the U.K. the government introduced a policy of permitting council property tenants to buy their rental properties, from the councils at a discount. Many have argued that the result of this policy is that the stock of affordable rental property for the poorer in society has been reduced significantly. This is true. It is to the shame of this country that the cost of renting a property is now so high that living in a property is such a strain for so many people, whether they rent or buy.

However, I have participated in this gold rush by advising my own clients in this environment. As an adviser I arranged legitimate loans against council homes, as well as arranging Buy to Let loans for my clients on second properties. I acted within the rules (where have we heard that phrase before—it was all within the rules, we have done nothing wrong), so I am part of this machine.

Northern Rock (and other lenders) simply met the desire of all of us, as a society, to have more bigger and better stuff. We wanted to fund a lifestyle that included, almost by right: higher education for our kids; holidays abroad; more expensive cars; more white goods; gadgets; second homes and so on and so forth…

Our inherent desire for stuff caused mortgage lenders and credit card companies to come up with easy lines of credit which, in turn, led to us wanting more stuff as it became more affordable through easy access to credit, which led to increased lines of credit, which led to us buying more stuff. So the cycle continued and the level of credit increased.

Keith Tondeur[xii] OBE, the founder of the charity: Credit Action, says this:

> We buy stuff that we don't need; with money that we don't have; in order to impress people that we don't even like.

This cycle of personal debt, that can so easily spiral out of control is just like the government whose level of debt is now well out of control. Individually we might operate on a far smaller scale than our government, but the principles are the same.

The government feels obliged to maintain our standard of living, irrelevant of the costs involved. Until now they have ignored the increasing level of debt. They have to maintain our living standards in order to be re-elected, so the structures of government become more and more impotent. Until now politicians have been unwilling to address the problems with any real solutions as we the electorate would

---

[xii] Keith Tondeur is a tireless campaigner on the issue of debt. He has many inspiring stories to tell and is a speaker that is well worth a listen. You can find out more about his work at: http://www.creditaction.org.uk

hate the tough medicine that is required.

No matter which party is in power they are currently faced with a possible total collapse of the economy. This is true of many nations worldwide. I believe that we are standing close to the precipice. Does the government and the banks have enough money to pour into the system in order to continue propping up the financial institutions…? Well, this remains to be seen.

Because of our own inherent desire for a more expensive lifestyle, was the credit that was offered to us a response to our hunger for more? Or is it true that the banking and financial institutions created lines of easy credit that, in turn, enabled us to consider a wealthier lifestyle? Was it the financial chicken or the hunger for the egg of stuff that came first?

No matter which came first, credit facilities, or the insatiable appetite for stuff—as with the National Debt—our individual level of borrowing has increased significantly to dangerous levels.

We need to take a closer look at these levels of credit and in particular the Sub-Prime Market and the role of the banks in this regard. In spite of what I have said about our corporate responsibility, in the next chapter we will come to see that the irresponsible lending of the banks is one of the major factors that has bought the world's economies crashing down about our ears? The question is, are we ready for further collapse and yet more fall-out affecting the markets generally?

CHAPTER FIVE

LEND US A TENNER MATE

So how much in debt are we, personally? We have looked at the debt of the government of the U.K.—and commented upon the fact that many other countries are in a similar state—but what about us, as individuals, how are we shaping up?

Let's look at some basic figures as at the end of April 2010:[xiii]

1. The level of total personal debt, in the U.K. stood at £1.460 billion (**this is now estimated as being over £1,000,000,000,000,000,000**—this is a whole lot of zero's—an increase of around £0.6 billion in a few months);
2. The level of total consumer credit lending to individuals, in the U.K. stood at around £221 billion;
3. Including mortgages, the average household debt in the U.K. was around £57,915.

And here are some further disturbing averages for the U.K.:

1. Every day the population pays, collectively, £186 million in personal interest;
2. Once, every 13.4 minutes a property is repossessed;
3. Once, every 51 seconds someone will be declared insolvent or bankrupt.

By the time you have read this far how many people will have been made homeless? It is also shocking—in this country—that if your home is repossessed by your mortgage company, you are often considered to have intentionally made yourself homeless. Is your own neighbour now on the street? If this is the case then the local authority is probably not legally bound to house them!

Our society is living so far outside of the boundaries of the Biblical principle of looking after the dispossessed. It is a shameful place to find ourselves. Furthermore—

[xiii] The source of these figures and statistics are from Credit Action. More details can be found at: http://www.creditaction.org.uk

in these circumstances of repossession—in order to grant the repossessed time to find more permanent accommodation a local authority may only have to provide temporary accommodation for no more than a month or so. After this period of time the council can request the dispossessed to leave the accommodation that they have provided, at any time. There is little protection from eviction for the repossessed in this country.

People can make stupid decisions in life (I have made a great deal of wrong turns in my life), and there can be resulting circumstances that are often detrimental financially. People may need to face up to the result of their actions, but, for our so called civilised society to have the possibility of allowing families; couples; single parents; their offspring; to become homeless and then do nothing to assist them, this is abhorrent in my view. If the government wishes to allocate some of the National Debt to assisting a specific sector of society that requires help, then this is surely one that deserves consideration!

One reason that I would argue for a safety net for those who cannot maintain their mortgage payments, is to support innovation and enterprise. History is littered with entrepreneurs, inventors, artists, composers failing, and then succeeding. Some would argue that it is the hardships that many have suffered that have given them fortitude and perseverance, but for me, supporting one another in both the good times and the bad seems to be an inherent mark of a civilised and Godly society, whether this be on a national or local level. Supporting those who become ill and are unable to work and therefore can no longer afford their mortgage repayments, is surely a mark of a just society and nation.

I can point out that in the pages of my arbitrator God was talking to and instructing a nation, a chosen people, who may have been small and insignificant at the time, but size is relative they say (lol), but this nation of Israelites was still a nation. God's laws were put into place for that chosen nation. He (that is God) wanted them to enact these laws of justice in order to try and enable them to be a beacon in a world of despair. Surely now, more than ever, the world needs a light of hope, a ray of financial stability and economic salvation. Personally I long for social justice to become a reality, nationwide, and within all sectors of society, rich, poor, middle class.

We need radical reform and change, but we don't need any more laws to govern us, we need compassion and justice. We have more than enough laws on the statute books to sink the Titanic. We require a total radicalisation of government and the manner in which politics is conducted. We need to learn patience as a people, granting those in power time to get things onto a stable footing. The cure is not as simple as blaming one sector of our society. The solution cannot be magicked up overnight. For the sake of a sick world, we need to embrace concepts of justice. We need to bring to the fore social justice to a degree that has never been seen in the history of this great nation.

As I have tried to outline, the figures show that as a society we have fallen into the trap of refinancing ourselves (just like the government and football) to a high degree. We may now require more and more capital just to meet interest payments. How often have you heard that someone is only able to pay the interest on their credit cards and that they are not paying off any capital? The other problem with the concept of consolidating debt is that there is no change to the inner person i.e. the human heart.

I was discussing a lot of this with a respected fund manager in the city of London, let's call him Derek. Our conversation went something like this:

Me: When I started working in the financial sector, I used to show mortgage clients the history of interest rates, and outline to people what would happen if the rates doubled or went down.

Derek: You must have been in the minority.

Me: I was probably in the minority of one. But do you know something, you eventually get sucked into the machine. Although I did nothing wrong, I started to change and eventually I stopped talking about these figures so much.

I also recall when my wife and I took out our very first mortgage. The adviser at the

Building Society produced an illustration that was an investment linked, endowment based mortgage. Towards the end of the interview, she shuffled across some papers and said something like:

> Here is another illustration.

She had in her hand a capital interest and repayment illustration, and she continued:

> I just have to show you this, but it is nothing really.

She then proceeded to shuffle the papers together, without giving us a chance to question her or to view the papers she had produced. We had no real chance to make a true comparison between an endowment and a repayment mortgage.

Was an endowment plan the best for us? In hindsight this probably was the best option, but I was not working in the financial services industry at the time. Neither I nor my wife knew which to choose. When I started working in the financial services sector I soon discovered that an endowment mortgage paid the highest amount of commission. I personally believe that some endowment plans were valid at the time. I still have one that covers part of my mortgage. But sometimes it was commission that drove the sale of endowment plans over that of a capital and interest repayment mortgage.

One of my own family members was advised to take out an endowment mortgage when they were past the age of 50, and the term was for 30 years; this meant that both the plan, and the mortgage would finish when they were in their eighties! I cannot fathom the thought process of the adviser; the advisers manager; the compliance department; and the lending company who offered the mortgage. Until stricter regulation was enforced this type of practice went largely unchecked.

In addition to the issue of mortgage debt there is also the aspect of lending via credit cards and personal loans. I recently applied for a credit card. Without asking I was issued a new card with a limit of £9,000. How is this possible when the lender has:

never met me;

assumed that I am telling the truth regarding my income;

assumed that I am telling the truth regarding my relationship with my wife—I could be married on paper only?

Granting such a high level of credit, based upon the information that I have supplied, combined with an online check with a credit reference agency, is both surprising, and worrying.

Earlier I explained that the government is recycling their line of credit and that their level of credit is increasing because they are borrowing money in order to meet the interest payments. With us, as individuals, it is a very similar pattern. In a conversation with my city friend Derek, just the other day, I was outlining this theory of refinancing credit. He agreed that many people may do this, but he added to this debate an interesting point that I think is very valid. He said the following:

> When people refinance their credit they tend to treat their credit cards and their personal loans as personal debt. They count it as theirs. They generally believe it to be a debt that they owe and at some stage these debts need to be repaid. When moving the accrued debts to the mortgage, that is a different story. Debt on a mortgage is no longer perceived to be a personal debt. It is a debt on the house and people do not see the mortgage as being like their credit card debt and personal loans. The mortgage is not seen as being personal. It is something that the house will take care of, sometime in the future. The problem only becomes personal, to most people, when they can no longer afford to pay the mortgage. That is the first time that it hits home. Their credit card debt and the personal loans that have all been added to the mortgage, are once again counted as being personal.

This is true (although I have no empirical data to prove this). It is an assessment derived from almost 20 years of working in the financial services sector. Advising on all of this stuff, I can say that there has been a lassez faire attitude to debt by many of us. The solution has been that our house and the surplus equity that we have within our homes would always be available to bail us out in hard times. There were no storm clouds on the horizon, it would always be sunny!

Before I become too critical I have to hold my hand up and say guilty as charged M'lud. I have overseen some of this refinancing of personal credit. I have helped clients to "wipe out" their debt—I am not advocating that I am 100% responsible for the credit crunch and the subsequent banking crisis, I am not that important—I am just pointing out my part in the massive machine. Many advisers I know did the same. My colleagues will be shocked to have any implication of irresponsibility being levied at them, but I ask their forgiveness. The vast majority of advisers that I know are honest and upright.

Perhaps many of us, whether we be an adviser; an individual seeking borrowing; a lending institution; the regulator; or a politician, we all need to assess our responsibilities within this crisis in order to move on. We also need to decide, as a society, as to what level of support the state should offer to those who have apparently, under the law, made themselves intentionally homeless!

The prospect of an ever increasing level in the price of property was (and is) unrealistic. Many of us have tended to maintain a belief that a property would increase in value forever—or at least that property prices were always going to drop tomorrow—and that there would never be a problem. This is proving to be extremely short sighted. With property prices in recent years, we have seen a market grow massively. Fortunes were made, until the boom went south!

I remember having many conversations with people. They were so excited that the property that they had purchased ten or fifteen years earlier, had doubled, trebled or even quadrupled. I always wondered what the fuss was about. If the home that you live in has gone up in value by so much, the next step up on the property ladder has also increased by a significant margin as it too has become more expensive. Despite this, the gold rush into property as a dead cert had begun.

There was also a new kid on the block. Landlords of no experience began to emerge. This new breed made the most of repossessed properties, buying property cheaply, renovating run down properties, then selling them on or renting them out.

There was also a new borrower. Those who had suffered personal financial losses and had bad debts against their names created a whole new market place almost overnight. The sub-prime market was born. As I have said, some lenders were willing to lend to anyone, no matter their credit history, income, or seemingly the value of their property. So now let's take a closer look at this lucrative market by turning our eyes, briefly, across the Atlantic Ocean and to one Fannie Mae and Freddie Mac:

> The institution, Fannie Mae, was created in 1938 as part of Roosevelt's: New Deal. The national housing market in the U.S. had utterly and totally collapsed in the wake of the great depression. Private lenders did not want to invest in the property market, Fannie Mae was founded to provide local banks with federal money to finance home mortgages. It was hoped that this would increase home ownership through affordable housing.
>
> Initially this enabled banks to charge low interest rates to home buyers for their mortgages. The secondary mortgage market was born. Companies like Fannie Mae, could borrow money from foreign investors at comparatively low interest rates because they received finances from the U.S. Government. This gave the perception of security through some form of government backed guarantees.
>
> Fannie Mae provided fixed interest rate loans, to home buyers, and low levels of deposits were accepted. Fannie Mae made profits from the difference between the interest rates that the borrowers paid, and that which foreign lenders charged.
>
> All appeared to be rosy. What homeowner with virtually no income, and very little deposit, could resist.
>
> For the first thirty years of its life, Fannie Mae had a monopoly in this unique market place. They enjoyed a unique position in the lending arena.
>
> In 1968, mainly due to the financial pressures that were created by the war in Vietnam, President Lyndon B. Johnson took this company out of the

national budget and state ownership and Fannie Mae was privatised. The company now began operating as a Government Sponsored Enterprise (GSE).

They generated profits for share holders while they enjoyed the amazing benefit of being exempt from taxation. There was no regulatory oversight. The line of government credit continued to be easy.

Eventually someone thought that, in the market economy of the land of the free, having a monopoly was a bad idea. A second GSE was formed in 1970 and this was known as Freddie Mac.

These two companies grew so rapidly that they eventually controlled around 90% of the secondary mortgage market in the U.S.

These GSEs—with their unique combination of both private enterprise and government backing and favourable tax treatment—experienced a period of fantastic growth over no more than a few decades. ***It is estimated that the assets of just these two companies, at one time, amounted to a total that was 45% greater than that of the largest bank in the U.S.*** But on the other hand, at the same time it was calculated that ***the combined debt of the two companies was the equivalent of 46% of the total National Debt of the U.S.***

Eventually concerns were voiced and questions were raised. Fannie Mae and Freddie Mac were the only two Fortune 500 companies that were not required to make public any financial difficulties that they were experiencing.

The concern was, if there was some sort of financial collapse within either of these companies, the U.S. taxpayers could be held responsible for hundreds of billions of dollars in outstanding debts.

An investigation by the Justice Department and the Securities Exchange Commission into the accounting practices at Freddie Mac revealed some worrying accounting errors, to the tune of $4.5 to $4.7 billion!

Heads rolled. Three of the company's top executives had to go. The U.S. Congress then stepped in and started a full investigation into the role of GSEs and the secondary (sub-prime) mortgage market.

These two mortgage companies, about the largest the world has ever seen, were estimated to be holding, or guaranteeing, some $5 trillion in debt! This is a far cry from the origins of Fannie Mae who began with just $1 billion in purchasing power.

The belief that loans of GSEs were backed by a government guarantee had generated the mistaken and misplaced belief that the U.S. government owned and backed them. The reality is that no GSE received any form of government guarantee.

When these two companies collapsed the repurcussions worldwide were enormous. Financial institutions throughout the world had loans tied up with these GSEs. Our pension funds and other investments were in part tied up in them, via complex financial products.

The ripple effect was simply unprecedented. Institutions woke up to the reality that there was no money in the pot and that U.S. government money was not available to prop them up. Great sighs of relief resounded, throughout the globe, when the U.S. administration did decide to step in and save the GSEs from utter melt down.

How were—in the main—just two companies allowed to get away with such a favourable taxation treatment, with implied government backing; no compliance oversight; no real auditing of accounts; no requirement to report any financial difficulties and the virtual monopolisation of the secondary (sub-prime) mortgage market?

The end result was inevitable. The housing market declined as approximately 80% of U.S. mortgages issued in the previous few years to sub-prime borrowers were on some type of variable rate and the loan repayments of the GSEs could not be met as interest rates rose. The U.S. government stepped in and bailed out the two largest GSEs. Effectively they took over the control of the companies. It has been reported that the U.S. Government has set aside a staggering $200 billion to prop up just these two companies!

History has gone full circle. The very foundation of Fannie Mae lies in the aim of propping up the housing market by the U.S. Government and the provision of low cost housing to the under-privileged. So history is now being repeated. How could we have learned so little from the past? Successive U.S. governments simply accepted the status quo, they permitted it to continue. Under the watch of some U.S. Presidents they actively encouraged these companies. There are also some accusations being levied that the GSEs gave money to political parties in order to prevent stricter regulation and oversight being bought in.

The GSEs had the opportunity to make money through a distortion of lending at artificially low rates. Just like other opportunities that fell across the path of others that I have outlined, this opportunity was grabbed eagerly with both hands by the GSEs and the institutional investors and the lenders. They wanted to make profits. Perhaps they should have asked more obvious questions, such as can we see some audited accounts before passing across many millions of our hard earned money to these GSEs!

Another extraordinary thing about this fiasco is that as GSEs—such as Fannie Mae and Freddie Mac—increased home ownership in the U.S. over the last fifty years or so without ever lending a single dime of their own money! They persuaded investors to provide money for mortgage loans, with a slick sales pitch that (some believed) amounted to an implied money-back guarantee. They promised investors that if borrowers defaulted they guaranteed to repay the investors from their own reserves. Rather than making actual loans from their own money these two companies gained loans from banks and other investors, thereby providing money for more lending.

There is an inherent flaw to this scheme. Where on earth does the money come from to make good the cast iron guarantees when it all goes wrong? The GSEs had no money, they were simply a conduit for the lending of money, a mere middle man, who paid returns to the investors who gave them money to lend!

Do you know the phrase: if it sounds too good to be true, then it is likely to be too good to be true? Why didn't alarm bells clang loudly in the ears of investors and institutional lenders? Institutions bypassed normal sensibilities and they handed over yours and mine hard earned cash in our pension schemes to the likes of Freddie and Fannie!

Fannie Mae once proudly declared, in its mission statement:
> Our business is the American dream of home ownership...

In the year 2001 the company set a target of helping to create six million new homeowners by 2014. In the state of Arizona, during the housing boom that was fuelled by cheap land and cheap borrowing, executives of Fannie Mae also announced that:
> ...the company would invest $15 billion to help families buy homes.

This honourable desire of Fannie and Freddie to apparently help the poor could not be met as increasingly they were channeling investors money into loans that borrowers could not afford. Defaults mounted and they quickly ran low on funds and they could not honour their guarantees. Repossessions increased as the economic downturn set in. A resident who lives in the Phoenix suburb of Avondale says that she has seen six of the nine homes that are visible from her chair on her lawn have been emptied by removal companies during the last year. Four of these properties have been resold by the government to new owners.

Yet here is the rub. The U.S. government effectively own a major share of these two GSEs, yet they are repossessing their own citizens of their own homes. What did the residents do wrong? They were sold the American dream of owning their home. They had secured a loan at a low rate of interest and now the baliffs are coming along and taking away their dream. How can this shameful practice continue in the country that is termed as the land of the free. It is the most powerful democracy on the planet? It is utterly and totally repugnant that the world has arrived at this point of depravity. What is even more despicable to me is that the U.S. claims to be a Christian country!

The rate of repossession is likely to continue. It is now reported that new home sales in 2010—in the U.S.—dropped by a massive 33% in May!

But this is also bad news for the U.S. government as it is reported that **Freddie and Fannie owns, or guarantees, half of all of the mortgages in the U.S.!** Pause for a moment to re-read the last sentence again.

In the first quarter of 2010 these two GSEs saw around 1,000 foreclosures a day! This equates to about one home in every 90 seconds! That's 91,000 repossessed homes, effectively by the U.S. government, in just three months.

A Democrat Senator, Chris Dodd said the following:

> Look, this program needs to be fixed. There's no question about it, you need an alternative housing finance system. That is without question.

Not everyone agrees with this analysis but I think that he has hit the nail on the head. The principle of having available to citizens, some form of low cost housing—whether this be through the likes of government backed loans, or through low rental—is a must. It is a good solid Biblical principle. In the U.K. we used to have something called Council Houses. This stock of housing was sold off. The dream of owning your own home was the very large carrot put in the front of tenants noses by the Thatcher gavernment of the 1980s.

In the U.S. and the U.K. the repossession of people's homes continues, despite banks and financial institutions being owned by governments, in part or in full! It is a dirty practice to effectively turf out your own citizens and then sell the homes of the repossessed from under their own noses. But wait, there is another part to the Freddie and Fannie story:

> An elderly woman, a client of Fannie Mae, shot herself and later died of the injuries that she sustained in her attempted suicide. Apparently she owed less than $50,000! When baliffs and representatives of the loan company called around to her home, she would hide inside her house and so a notice was posted onto her door. The sad irony is that they eventually decided not to pursue the debt and the company forgave the loan.

The executives of the GSEs are not exempt from pressure and subsequent loss:

In 2009 it was reported that the Chief Financial Officer (CFO) of Freddie Mac was found dead, apparently having committed suicide. This is just a month after he was given a controversial $850,000 retention bonus, while he tried to dig the lender out of the financial quagmire.

Digging a little deeper and when examining the suicide of this executive, it was also reported that:

> Mr. Kellerman, 41, began working non-stop, sometimes returning home only to change clothes, colleagues said. He was losing weight and telling friends that it seemed impossible to appease everyone—regulators, lawmakers, investors and other executives—given their competing demands. Someone was always angry with him, he told one friend. And, continued his friend, no matter how many hours everyone worked, it seemed as if the economy and homeowners were still slipping further into the abyss.[xiv]

The following is what a blogger called Kirsten said of David Kellerman's death:[xv]

> This just goes to show the toll corporate America takes on us all. I'm a lower middle class waitress stressing out to pay the bills making $3.31 per hour plus a few tips. This man just received a $850,000 bonus and didn't want to continue living his extravagant life. Money doesn't bring happiness, but it shouldn't bring upon death either.
>
> Kellerman was placed in a highly stressful position and had to basically sit back and watch as his company let millions of Americans become homeless due to poor decision making—poor decision making made by his predecessors, not Kellerman.
>
> He leaves behind a wife and a small child—all for what—because corporate America behaved badly for a few years and this innocent man had to shoulder a huge load of the blame. We all have bad days at work, but when a bad day

---

[xiv] The source of this report is: http://www.nytimes.com/2009/04/23/business/23freddie.html
[xv] This blog can be read in full at: http://www.askdeb.com/blog/news/david-kellerman/

at work forces you to take your life, what kind of job is that?

…This is just another tragedy in the endless string of misery, pain, and misfortune the collapse of Wall Street has brought to all Americans.

Let Kellerman's death be a reminder…Let's stop the greed, the blame game, and the finger-pointing; let's all take responsibility for our actions and help out our neighbours.

Who do you feel most sorry for. The borrower, or the well paid executive of the large conglomerate? It is also reported that David Kellerman's company managed to continue trading as normal and they bought and sold around 8,500 mortgages on the day of his death! This frenetic activity was only interrupted by a meeting at 11 a.m. for any employees who wished to pause and share memories of their deceased colleague.

What state are we in, in the West, when a firm continues to function completely normally in its role despite the reporting of the sad death of one of their top executives? What state are we in when the largest Western democracy in the world is pursuing the repossession of homes, from its own citizens, that result in the suicide of humble home owners who have essentially done nothing wrong?

What state are we in when complex lending is integrated into investment products that are basically rubbish (I will expand upon this in more detail shortly)?

Where is the integrity of politicians who were embroiled in the expenses scandal of the U.K.? (We do not yet know the full extent of the abuses within the EEC—I suspect that the story of moral corruption is rife throughout the world—I wonder if any institution or political movement of today, is exempt from corruption.)

What of the lending and financial institutions and their lending policies?

What of us? Have we hungered for too long, too hard and for too much? Can anyone claim any shred of decency within all of this mess?

[11]Do not withold your mercy from [us], O LORD; may your love and your truth always protect [us].

[12]For troubles without number surround [us];

> ^{13}[our] sins have overtaken [us], and [we] cannot see.
> They are more than the hairs of [our] head,
> and [our] heart[s] fail within [us].[xvi]

Have our sins now overtaken all of us, as a collective society? Perhaps we are now reaping simply what we have sown!

I have also spent some time wondering what the family of Mr. Kellerman thought as they have read and heard the incessant headlines about Bankers bonuses and irresponsible lending? And what of the family of that elderly woman who took her own life over her mortgage debt? I also wonder what they think of large bonuses given to so called Bankers such as Mr. Kellerman now?

These are just two examples behind the scapegoating headlines of recent times.

As I have said there are consequences to our actions. But there can be a deep personal cost for some that is well beyond that of being a financial one. This is a cost that simply cannot be measured against the value of our pension funds, savings and investments. I think that now may be a good time to recall the words of John Donne:

> No man is an island, entire of itself...any man's death diminishes me, because I am involved in mankinde...[xvii]

There are so many examples of irresponsibility and negligence that we could look at. Here is just one more. This company was the fifth-largest U.S. investment bank!

> 1923: The company Bear Stearns is founded by three people Joseph Bear, Robert Stearns and Harold Mayer with $500,000 in capital.
>
> 1969: A bridge tournament is being held in New York. At this tournament

---

[xvi] The Book of Psalms, Chapter 40 and verses 11 - 12.
[xvii] Taken from: Meditation XVIII by John Donne, 1572-1631. Donne was an English poet, preacher and an important representative of the period. His works are often noted for having a realistic and sometimes rather sensual style. His work includes: sonnets; love poems; religious poems; Latin translations; epigrams; elegies; songs; satires and sermons.

the future head of Bear Stearns, one Alan "Ace" Greenberg, happens to bump into the 35 year old Jimmy Cayne who was a professional card player at this time. (This is probably the root of the problem for this company.) Greenberg is apparently so impressed by the presence and courage of Cayne that he offers him a job, at Bear Stearns, as a stockbroker there and then.

1985: The bank seems to have made it. It becomes a publicly traded company.

March 2002: The gambling days of the now Chief Executive Officer (CEO), James Cayne, are not forgotten as the New York Sun announces that he will be writing a regular bridge column for the newspaper.

January 12th 2007: Bear Stearns shares close at a record $171.51 on momentum from its strong earnings report the previous month. The staff pop the champagne corks at this good news.

May 24th 2007: Bear Stearns shares close at $147.55. This is a six-week low. Goldman Sachs slashed its quarterly earnings target for the rival investment bank as it cites concerns it has about Bear Stearns' heavy exposure to mortgage securities business.

June 14th 2007: Bear Stearns reports that its earnings have declined for the first time in four quarters on weaker results from its mortgage securities business.

June 15th 2007: The Wall Street Journal, reports that a hedge fund run by Bear Stearns has suffered big losses. A second hedge fund will soon follow suit.

June 16th 2007: The Wall Street Journal reports that Merrill Lynch, a creditor to this losing hedge fund, seized some of its own assets.

Late June 2007: Bear Stearns finds $3.2 billion to bail out two hedge funds that had been created to invest in the sub-prime mortgage market.

Mid July 2007: Losses from sub-prime mortgages begin to threaten credit markets around the world. Bear Stearns is exposed, heavily. The company decides to write to their clients to inform them that these two hedge funds now contain "very little" or "effectively no value" for investors. Bear Stearns shares end the day at $139.91.

August 2007: Both of the bust hedge funds run by the bank file for bankruptcy.

October 5th 2007: Prosecutors launch a criminal probe into the collapse of the two Bear Stearns hedge funds. The stock closes at $131.58.

October 2007: The CEO, Cayne issues statements of reassurance to their investors. He says:

> Most of our businesses are beginning to rebound.

Later the same month, the state-owned Chinese lender Citic pays $1 billion for a 6% stake in Bear Stearns. This has the effect of giving the firm a value of approximately $20 billion. (Why anyone wanted to invest at this stage is beyond me.)

December 2007: The company reports a fourth-quarter loss of $854 million. This is due to massive mortgage-related failures. This is the very first quarterly loss in the 85 year history of the bank.

January 2008: Cayne is virtually forced to resign as CEO. This resignation follows a Wall Street Journal article that revealed his recreational use of pot; his appetite for month long vacations to play cards; amongst other colourful activities. The board kept Cayne on as its chairman, appointing Alan D. Schwartz as the new CEO.

March 12th-13th 2008: Responding to these market rumors that the institution is close to collapse and that it has severe liquidity problems, the CEO Schwartz goes on a public-relations offensive. He appears on CNBC TV and he assures viewers by saying:

> We don't see any pressure on our liquidity, let alone a liquidity crisis…

Despite his attempts at trying to boost confidence the perception of the company being in trouble soon becomes a reality. Institutional investors and hedge fund managers want their money and they get out.

Friday night, March 13th-14th 2008: The executives are now desperate. They have no money to operate their business. They put in an all-nighter trying to work out what to do. Eventually at 5.00 am they wake up the Federal Reserve chairman, Ben Bernanke, with a phone call. They discuss the crisis with him, and other advisers. They come up with a rescue plan. They do a deal with JPMorgan and the Federal Reserve Bank of New York. It is the largest bail-out, ever, of a U.S. based securities firm. The share price of Bear Stearns is shot to pieces, they fell by 47% to close at just $30 a share.

The concern of the Chairman and previous CEO was there for all to see. Jimmy Cayne, when faced with the potential collapse of the 85 year old venerable institution, allegedly he went back to his first love. It is reported that he took part in a bridge tournament in Detroit!

March 16th–17th, 2008: After forcing a raft of Bankers to work over the weekend JPMorgan decides to buy Bear Stearns, but only with Federal Reserve backing. The going price was just $2 a share. The revaluation of the once giant firm is now just $236 million, that is a reduction from the peak of an estimate of $6 billion.

What do you think? Were the high rolling bridge players really worth the bonuses? What of the statements of reassurance by the highly paid executives. Could they really have not known what was about to happen? Before you answer; please bear in mind that this company—prior to their collapse—had gained such a good reputation in the markets that it was a recognised authority for market news. So much so that it published news that was widely read in publications called: Early Look at the Market—Bear Stearns Morning View, which was accompanied by: Morning Meeting Packet.

This company was the top notch company for intelligent news. Much store was placed upon the insights of this firm. This investment house was once recognised as the "Most Admired" securities firm in Fortune's "America's Most Admired

Companies" survey. This annual survey is very prestigious and it ranks: employee talent; the quality of risk management; business innovation etc… Look again at what this survey specifically measures. Employee talent and the quality of risk management! This is laughable when you consider what happened. And, they won this distinction three years running. Some have joked that Fortune must have been paid by Bear Stearns to give the award in the third and final year.

In the closing of this chapter, I hope that you can see that there are some, like Kellerman who, according to his colleagues, tried his damndest to do the best that he could in an impossible situation. We then have another city breed. A breed that are in reality no more than high rolling card players, literally playing with our savings and investments in order to gain high bonuses. And these high rollers were patted on the back by a respected journal because they were reckoned to be the best in their field and these awards were given just prior to the gamblers allowing an 85 year old bank collapse. The reason that this firm went under is due to ignorance; negligence; greed; and high rolling players playing foot-loose and fancy-free with investors money.

The collapse of this banking institution (and they are not alone) was simply abject greed. They were exposed to a market downturn that was not foreseen. Yet these guys were awarded top echelon awards as they were meant to be the cream of the crop. These awards must mean nothing. They are just the chance to pat others on the back. When I receive the annual industry awards for life, investment and pension companies I put the voting slips in the bin. They are not worth the paper that they are written on.

In all these collapsing companies that we have examined, albeit briefly, whether it be the GSEs or old institutions, those at the top failed to predict the downturn in the sub-prime markets. When they did, they either took little to no effective action, and at best they were mistaken in their belief that they could survive, at worst they simply lied in the media and on national TV. The truth is that they could not do anything about it as it was simply too late. They were utterly impotent.

Who do I mean by those at the top? I refer to the CEO's of the city firms; the fund managers; all of these combined into a toxic pot that had failure written all over it. But I also refer to legislators and regulators. There was too much freedom and latitude.

This chapter has chiefly been about the sub-prime market. This failed market place has been a major contributory factor to the global crisis that has come about for when this market place failed, the markets toppled, like a house of cards.

So what warnings does my arbitrator give about lending. In the book of Proverbs, Chapter 22 and verse 7 it says:

> The rich rule over the poor,
>   and the borrower is slave to the lender.

For too long we have been slaves and the financial institutions have been making more slaves for one thing and one thing only. A large level of profit, and not just for themselves. The current lending practice and resulting investment markets are totally contrary to that which is outlined in the Bible. Look at Psalm 37 and verse 26:

> He will make your righteousness shine like the dawn, the justice of your cause like the noonday sun.

Is there anything righteous about the lending policies of the GSEs and so many other institutions? Then we read Psalms, Chapter 112 and verse 5:

> Good will come to him who is generous and lends freely, who conducts his affairs with justice.

The scriptures go yet further in book of Deuteronomy, Chapter 15:

> [1]At the end of every seven years you must cancel debts. [2]This is how it is to be done: Every creditor shall cancel any loan they have made to a fellow Israelite. They shall not require payment from anyone among their own people, because the Lord's time for cancelling debts has been proclaimed. [3]You may require payment from a foreigner, but you must cancel any debt your fellow Israelite

owes you. ⁴However, there need be no poor people among you, for in the land the LORD your God is giving you to possess as your inheritance, he will richly bless you, ⁵if only you fully obey the LORD your God and are careful to follow all these commands I am giving you today.

When reading the Holy Bible, it is quite clear, that as a model, lending with interest within the community of the nation of Israel was forbidden. Furthermore, there was, at the time, a periodic cancellation of debt. God also declares that a mark of a Godly society is one where there are no poor among them.

In scripture we must be careful about applying a principle of yesterday's culture, to that of today. These laws, proverbs and poetry are not necessarily blueprints to be exactly copied. They must be interpreted in the light of the culture at the time, and then see how can we apply the same principles today. For example, if lending was interest free from tomorrow, your investments would be hit like a tornado and decrease in value markedly. I do not believe that this is what God would want, but however literally you apply these verses there is an underlying principle of fairness within the text and it is do not allow people to live in poverty through your lending practices, and certainly do not repossess them.

What has happened in society and the modern day mortgage is the relationship of trust between the borrower and the lender has become divorced from one another. Your mortgage debt may be money that has come through 5, 6, 7 or 8 different lenders before it is leant to you. All those lenders are expecting a cut of the profits. Therefore the one to one personal relationship, and the relationship of trust has been wiped out from your transaction. In the times of the Israelites, lending was based upon a relationship of trust between just two parties.

I have not got time to dwell upon alternative forms of Biblical lending, in full, I leave that to the experts, but there are different Biblical concepts of lending that are interest free. These are outlined within the text of scriptures. Sharing in business profits, is but one example. But, when considering these principles we have the likes of the South Sea Bubble, or Ponzi and Madoff (more on all of this later), whereby the corruption of man's heart prevents even these alternative lending and investment schemes from working.

Under the current lending structures, we have seen the boom, and now we are experiencing the consequences of the bust. A lecturer and speaker on these issues, one Paul Mills, outlines that we have seen the worst rise in unemployment in the U.S. since WWII, and that there has been a 40% fall in house prices in the U.S. and now 21% of borrowers are in negative equity. These figures are shocking. Behind every redundancy and repossession there are real lives, not just statistics, but real lives of real people who are being allowed to live in poverty in a so called Christian country.

Trust between lender and borrower is shot to pieces. We now need liberation from the bondage that the Holy Bible speaks of. No matter which way you dress it up, borrowing money makes you into a slave to the lender. Think about it. Your opportunity to move freely can be curtailed by the loan that you have upon a property. Your ability to rent out your property to family members is restricted under the lending criteria of lenders in the U.K. To have people living in your property is not up to you, it is down to the lender to determine the rules upon who can and who cannot live in the property, especially when they are over the age of 18.

This type of slavery is condemned in scripture. How we can eke ourselves out of this mire of unfairness is a struggle that is facing the modern world? How can we be fair to investors, lenders and borrowers alike? I believe that a time will come when the slaves to the banks and lending institutions will be set free. I also have a haunch that we are yet to see the full level of devastation that will arrive as a consequence of past flawed policies. We are not yet even in the centre of this storm, it is yet to blow out. How violent this storm will be no-one can foretell. All we can do is beg God to stay his hand and look upon us with mercy.

Let's look at this slavery in a little more detail and God's response to it. We shall learn that abject greed and that the repossession of property, which is contrary to the law of God, is nothing new.

CHAPTER SIX

POSSESSION IS NINE TENTHS OF THE LAW

> [1]Woe to those who plan iniquity, to those who plot evil on their beds! At morning's light they carry it out because it is in their power to do it. [2]They covet fields and seize them, and houses, and take them. They defraud a man of his home, a fellow-man of his inheritance.

I wonder if you recognise these words? You might guess that they come from the Holy Bible, my arbitrator, but where in the scriptures might we find them? They are the words of someone who is called a minor prophet, his name was Micah.

We have seen in the last chapter how a co-ordinated system of lending abuse has led to the marked growth in the repossession of property. The situation in the U.K. may not be quite the same, but according to latest figures—as I have previously mentioned—*one home in the U.K. is repossessed on average every 13.4 minutes.* This is a shocking indictment of the combination of our hunger to own our homes; the bad lending decisions of the financial institutions; poor regulation by government and utter ineptitude by politicians. When reviewing this current crisis I hope that I have established that we share a corporate responsibility for what has occurred. The solution to prevent this from happening again is in all of our hands.

Sadly, this whole arena of injustice in the repossessing of houses and land is nothing new. Many hundreds of years ago the prophet Micah was prophesying against this injustice to the people of God. I am certain that every human community that has ever lived has been subject to corruption and not just the nation of Israel. As the Holy Bible is my arbitrator further examination of this text is warranted.

In the days of this little known prophet violence was being used to seize property. Justice had been abandoned and perverted. Commercial and contractual abuse was commonplace, deceit is evident, family life is distorted, moral and social evils are prevalent, the equivalent of government—the religious leaders and the judges—could be bought. Does this sound any different from many societies of today? Is anything like this happening in our own Western world? There are some marked similarities that we can take note of within this ancient book.

The capital city of Northern Kingdom of Israel, Samaria, had already fallen to invaders. Micah used this as a warning to the Southern city, Jerusalem, and the people of Judah. He pulled no punches in his words. He spoke as someone with conviction as to what would happen to the people of the South if they did not change their ways.

From our vantage point, we can see that there is a temporary stay of God's retribution. Initially the people heeded the words of the prophet Micah, they repented, but he knew that they would soon fall back into their old ways. His words became a message of hope for the remnant of Israel who were left desolate, post subjugation and invasion.

This is the background to this little book in the scriptures. I now wish to concentrate upon the abuse of the repossessing of property and land of the tenants that is outlined by Micah.

Under the leadership of the King, named Uzziah, there had been a dramatic economic recovery in the nation of Israel. Micah started his rebuke with the simple word: Woe. In the time of Micah this word was used at funerals as a cry of grief. He then combined this mournful shout with the familiar saying of: If the cap fits, wear it! You are evil, you plot repossession on your beds, he told them. He revealed that the wealthy landowners were carefully planning the eviction of their tenants—fellow men, women and children, of the chosen nation of Israel—and all of this was carried out under the guise of governance.

The landlords were so intent upon amassing wealth that they had devised various means of gaining more wealth (a bit like the Bankers of recent times—who devised complex products solely for profit). The landowners must have had sleepless nights because they were up all hours scheming ways of how they could evict those who failed to maintain their rental payments.

Wealth had flowed into the land, but it was for the benefit of the few. Riches were not distributed evenly during the time of boom. The poor remained poor, the rich got richer, and as such they grew in power and influence.

Does any of this sound familiar? Not just for our own nation, but on a global scale?

In the days of Micah this relatively new rich class had more money than they knew what to do with. But this wealth had been accrued in a dishonest manner. There was a desire for the wealthy to acquire more and more. My city friend, Derek said to me the other day:

> Do you realise that enough is never enough. Why is it that many wealthy people continue to work? We might admire the charitable work and the foundations that the wealthy set up, but you can bet that they are still working to acquire even more wealth.

I like the simple words of Keith Tondeur, the founder of Credit Action, I once heard him comment something like:

> It used to be that your mum would tuck the label of your jumper in, but now we all want to wear the label of the maker of our clothes on the outside, for everyone to see as a badge of status.

The state of the human heart is poor. Enough never appears to be enough. What is more, status symbols are everything. In the days of Micah, they were prepared to defraud a man of his home! Repossession was commonplace, the landowners were unscrupulous. Micah had witnessed the social problems that were caused by the loss of traditional family small-holdings that had been replaced with large estates. The very infrastructure of the nation had changed dramatically. The number of dispossessed, hard working farmers was growing. If they had a bad season and their crops failed; if they could not pay the mortgage; then they had their very homes snatched from underneath them.

Today an illness may strike at the heart of a family. The main breadwinner many have no salary—or a reduced level of income—and no means of repaying their mortgage? Or perhaps a business fails, the sales orders are reduced—especially in the economic climate of today.

Micah was not solely concerned with the ever widening gap between the rich and the poor. He saw the cruel injustice that accompanied this practice of the enforced repossession of property and the destitution that resulted. The condition of the Israelite society at large highlighted a moving away from the religious practice of adhering to the teaching of a most high and just God.

Micah proclaimed that the landowners coveted land and wealth. This is extremely strong language. Coveting was (and is) a clear breach of the laws of Moses. Coveting is forbidden in scripture and Micah highlights that the landowners were displaying a clear disregard of this divine law. They had moved from a state of justice, to injustice, and by doing so they had rejected the ancient laws of God.

The people of God had also been taught that the land belongs to God. The people were stewards of the land. As keepers of the land they were instructed that the Land was not to be transferred to others. Read with me in the book of Leviticus, Chapter 25:

> [23]The land must not be sold permanently, because the land is mine and you are but aliens and my tenants.

I am not advocating that in modern day society land and property should not be mortgaged, but there is a principle here. For the person of faith, our property and possessions are transitory; we must place our eyes upon the permanency and eternal concept of heaven. For the unbeliever, I can only proffer an old saying:

> You can't take it with you!

There is also the common sense practice of justice. Is it an act of justice to take the home away from a family when they are ill, or have been made redundant, or when their business is failing? Is this really an honourable form of governance? After almost 20 years of working within the financial services sector, I question the entire lending and advisory system. (I am a slow learner.)

The current systems that are in place, should we experience a deeper economic downturn, seem to be inherently unfair.

On the other hand, there are consequences to action, and inaction. If a bank does not repossess a property when the owners are in default on their mortgage repayments, the bank will lose money; do this too many times and the share price of the bank will go down; our pension funds will be adversely affected; the cycle of poverty will continue into retirement.

The solutions are far from simple. I do not pretend to know the answer, we may need to sit with economists; Bankers; politicians; regulators and the prophets of today; around a table to come up with a cohesive answer, that is equitable to all.

There are further implications to the repossession of homes. With society failing to operate a decent safety net, families can be left to sink or swim. I also believe that the faith communities—I can only speak of the one of which I am member—also have a role to play in the whole arena of social justice. I am unsure as to whether the church is ready to step up to the mark that is going to be required of them. A friend of mine, Mike Resch, (who happens to be a vicar) posted onto facebook the other day:

> Mike Resch thinks that most churches are more into Market Share...

I think that Mike has a point. Many churches are more concerned with how many are attending services, or the day to day running of their church rather than social justice. I once heard tell of a church that, not so long ago, had a meeting to seek God's will and purpose. The whole meeting revolved around what should be the colour of the new crockery for the tea and coffee that was being served post service!

The amount of discussion in churches that centres around the incidentals such as: the format of services; the styles of worship; the version of the Holy Bible that should be used; and many other matters. All of this discussion is out of proportion to the time that churches give over to what really matters. It is safer to talk about these internal matters than to turn and face the dirty horrible stuff that goes on outside of the church. More air time is often given over to the infrastructures within churches than it might give over to social care and justice within the villages, towns and cities in which a church community resides.

There are exceptions, and I am not condemning all churches out of hand, but when was the last time your local church (no matter the denomination) had a member of their congregation invite a homeless family to stay with them? When was the last time a local church paid for the housing of a homeless person? This is before we move onto meeting the needs of the rejected of society such as—let's take an example of Yeshua (Jesus)—prostitutes that he willingly ate with and conversed with. Imagine having a weekly lunch for prostitutes in your local church, perhaps offering free condoms, and—in the longer term—establishing a protection system and an escape route away from pimps and drug dealers. What about the alcoholics and the drug addicts in your area? Do they need help to kick their habit? The need for this type of care and social justice knows no bounds and it cuts across all classes. A handful of churches are engaged in social justice, but how many? I believe that if a church is not involved in social justice, in both their local (and the worldwide) community they are failing the gospel of Christ. So please allow me to ask this question, irrelevant of whether you are a member of the church that is down the road from you or not, but: ***would you notice if your local church shut down tomorrow?***

For me, I get excited when Lucy opens up a church tea rooms, to give space to people in need in her area. I love it when Steve, gets involved in the plight of the homeless. My heart quickens when John tells me of stories about how he is helping his clients through a local CAP (Christians Against Poverty) debt counselling service, releasing them from the stranglehold of debt through this free of charge service. I love seeing Patrick, engaging in the plight of the poverty stricken farmers—and the orphans—in Maseno, in Africa, by bringing practical teaching and help to this community, resulting in an environment of hope and independence where there was once hopelessness. I pray for Brian and Ann, who are local councillors, giving up their free time to be passionate about matters that affect the local community. I do not really care two hoots about their party political allegiance, it is more about two people who are engaged in issues of the local community, doing their damndest to improve matters. What of the pastor, Will, who wants to help those who have—or are—struggling with mental health issues? They are helped through difficult times through his organisation: Mind & Soul. What of Allie, the single hard working mum, who is looking at innovative ways of gaining work for carers in local businesses. I also appreciate the passion of Godfrey, setting up a sound system, when he (and his un-named team) dedicate hours and hours of willing service, behind the scenes, thereby bringing decent technology into a once redundant building enabling a church community to witness and worship!

All of this is the calling of the church. The response of humble, silent, souls, who do so much behind the scenes, always fills me with amazement and gratitude. They are looking outward beyond the walls of their building and not inwards, dreaming a dream, fulfilling their passions and wanting to bring practical justice and practical assistance in a world that is corrupt and unjust due to the fallen nature of the human heart.

On a national level, I have come to expect little of politicians in power nationally. Perhaps they are so far removed from reality. Institutionalised if you like. Politics today is a career where you can rise to the top and become a multi-millionaire owning a property portfolio beyond the dreams of most of us. One questions the motives of such politicians who declare that they are in it for the people such as you and I.

Likewise, with the national leaders of the faith communities, in the whole of the economic crisis of recent years, where were the "prophets" of today? Did they speak out about the flawed lending policies of the financial institutions? Where are their voices now? Do they now cry out against injustice, unafraid of the inevitable ridicule that will be heaped upon them? Micah was prepared to speak out. Are the teachers, preachers and prophets of today prepared to speak out against abhorrent practices of repossessing the poor? Or, are they more concerned about issues such as homosexuality, women priests, or even the teacups in their local churches, rather than social justice? I know of one "prophet" who foresaw the collapse of the markets, and said so, quite publicly. The likes of Keith Tondeur, and the founder of CAP, John Kirkby, have also worked to alleviate and prevent debt and they have both commented upon the many aspects of debt, but that's about it! I also consider my own financial advice community. What were we, the Christian financial advisers doing, and saying? Did we voice any concerns, or were we happy with the status quo? Many questions to which I am unable to find a satisfactory answer.

As an example for the politician and the prophet alike, Micah was overtly concerned with social justice. In the second chapter of his prophecy, he condemns the attitudes of the rich. Please note, as I have said earlier, he does not condemn wealth, but he does condemn the actions of the wealthy and the lack of social care within his faith community. In this chapter of the prophet's book, Micah speaks of the consequences of the abusive actions of the wealthy. This bit takes a step of faith, but please bear with me on this one:

> [3] Therefore, the Lord says:
> "I am planning disaster against this people, from which you cannot save yourselves.
> You will no longer walk proudly, for it will be a day of calamity.
> [4] In that day men will…taunt you with this mournful song:
> 'We are utterly ruined;
> my people's possession is divided up.
> He takes it from me!
> He assigns our fields to traitors.'"

No matter how much or how little faith you might have, and as I have said before, there is a consequence to our actions, it has always been the case and it will always be so.

No matter what you think of the spiritual element of the calamity that befell the people of Israel, there is something significant in the whole story that is outlined by Micah. There is a consequence to their actions beyond their reality. I believe that for us, here and now, there is a spiritual dimension to our activity here on this earth.

There is the saying: that what goes around, comes around, or: every dog has its day. This is the case here. Earthly wealth is transitory, it cannot bring salvation or comfort when things go wrong. The prophet makes this abundantly clear. In the event of the forthcoming invasion by foreign forces, the accumulated worldly wealth of the landowners is like a chocolate teacup. Entirely useless.

For us, here and now, I believe that we need to re-learn the prophetic words of Micah. These are words that echo and resound with truth down the ages as a warning to us, even today. We may have averted disaster, for now, in the financial markets, but have conditions really improved to such an extent that we no longer live in danger of total and utter financial collapse?

We must learn, re-learn, and educate our children, and we need to pass on the message to our children's children the valuable lesson that wealth is nothing; it is useless; it cannot bring any form of comfort when over-run by extreme disaster and perhaps it is far more difficult to lose a lot, than to lose virtually nothing, so why build up and store wealth and stuff? Read again the wise words of the Apostle Paul, in the book of 1 Timothy, Chapter 6:

> [17]Command those who are rich in this present world not to be arrogant nor to put their hope in wealth, which is so uncertain, but to put their hope in God, who richly provides us with everything for our enjoyment. [18]Command them to do good, to be rich in good deeds, and to be generous and willing to share. [19]In this way they will lay up treasure for themselves as a firm foundation for the coming age, so that they may take hold of the life that is truly life.

This scripture speaks of wealth being transitory. It also talks of being generous with wealth. If we do this we may then truly take hold of life itself! Our hearts need transformation. We need to view the provision of wealth as being part of God's rich and generous provision. It is HIS, and not ours. We are stewards who can enjoy the benefit of wealth but we must keep our eye on the greater prize, life itself, and all that this entails! This teaching of the Apostle is about humility, our maintaining a thankful heart, and this will result in generosity. Once we divert our eyes from heavenly generosity we are likely to become corrupted as our values will become distorted.

Micah also warned his listeners that they would not be able to walk proudly in the light of the corruption around them. The rich believed in walking proudly. In the context of the time, the act of walking proudly reflects the conduct of the wealth gatherers. The lifestyle and the identity of these people was measured by their peers, in accordance with the size of an individuals wealth. They have been so proud of their achievements that they were basking in the glory of riches, irrelevant of how they had been gained. They were walking with their heads held high, with abject pride. Their entire body language said look at me, look at my success, aspire to be like me. This is no different to the excesses of the city today. The fast living and high spending lifestyle of some (not all) city workers is no different in attitude of wealth = importance.

There is a warning from the prophet to his nation state. What is about to befall them was going to bring them down very low. It was God's purpose that it should be so. As if the cheating, deception and social injustice was not enough, there is another matter that Micah addresses, in the same chapter:

> [6]"Do not prophesy," their prophets say.
> "Do not prophesy about these things;
> disgrace will not overtake us."

Micah speaks out, quite forcefully against the biggest abuse. The rich and oppressive classes are not alone, they have their advocates and influential supporters. Believe it, or believe it not, the other so called prophets are saying:

> Don't preach at me, or at us. God will never do what you are saying. God has promised to look after us, we have a covenant promise in place with our God. There is no consequence to our actions. Just like the Titanic (obviously the Israelites didn't know of the Titanic at the time, but I hope you get my drift), we are unsinkable, for we live under God's protectorate therefore we can do anything that we like.

It is important to understand that the prophets and the judges were the arbitrators on points of the laws and justice at the time. They were the government, the equivalent of the House of Lords. For the right price, they could be bought. (I wonder where we have heard that before—a peer of the realm being paid to prophesy—ask questions.) In Micah's time bribery was on a mass scale. The false prophets were effectively saying:

> Ignore that useless prophet Micah, but listen to me instead; I will chat to you over a decent meal—and a beer—I will tell you all that you need to know. I will give you reassurance that all will be well, but Micah tells the truth, he says:
>
> [11]If a liar and deceiver comes and says, 'I will prophesy for you plenty of wine and beer,' then he would be just the prophet for this people!

I am not accusing the entire financial institutions of corruption, but the cities where billions are traded on a daily basis have little time for a God of mercy and provision. He is not on their radar. Instead, wealth and profits are to be worshipped. Make money is the hymn of praise that rises up in the city, as we will come to learn. But, as Al Jolson said in the first ever words of a movie:

> Wait a minute, wait a minute. You ain't heard nothin' yet!

At the time of Micah the prophets had stopped listening to the God of justice. They then rejected the sole true prophet of God. They believed that disaster would not come, the boom years were there to stay as they believed that they were operating under the promise of the most high and merciful God. As a God of promises, he would never go back on his word they believed. They continued to maintain this stance even when their neighbours, in the Northern city of Samaria, had been overrun by the foreign invaders. They believed in their own publicity. So it is today. We in the West cannot perceive that the fall of the Western markets and our historic democracies will ever occur. If it all goes wrong, we will be able to control it, and we will fix it. We can just throw money at the problem, it will be O.K. because we are rich and blessed! Micah holds this view in utter contempt, you can read the sarcasm in his words as he is effectively saying that:

You get what you deserve, and you have bought the opinion of the corrupt prophets and judges (the politicians and law makers) so very cheaply. It cost you the price of a bottle of wine or a few pints of beer!

That is how cheap the message of justice had become at the time of Micah. Surrounded by extremities of the boom of wealth, many had succumbed to buying a perverted word of God. The financiers of today may not have succumbed to corrupting the word of God, but as a society both they, and we, have failed to acknowledge or relate God to our wealth and to his merciful provision. We are invincible, has been the mantra of our economic downfall.

Similar attitudes in believing that boom was sustainable and impregnable rose up in the U.K. in the 1980s when many experienced an incredible growth in wealth. You could almost touch, taste and smell it. What is more, everyone wanted a piece of it. Rather arrogantly, few of us ever believed that it would end.

We then saw the bubble burst. The politicians then wanted to oversee the total elimination of boom and bust as they wanted to cancel it out and prevent it from ever happening again. Such naivety. As if the politicians could ever cancel out the inherent deficiencies of mankind that have been in evidence since the days of Micah, and earlier!

This prevalent arrogance towards wealth, and this belief that there is always a quick buck to be made has always been there. We don't have to go as far back as the times of Micah to see this in action. Mankind never learns. You may have heard of the South Sea Bubble. Here is a summary of this folly:

> In 1711 the British government had got themselves into the mire of debt. Within this context, some merchants clubbed together and formed a company called the: South Sea Trading Company. They bought around £10,000,000 of this government debt. They believed that they would gain a guaranteed annuity return of six percent, or around £570,000 annually.
>
> The government would then impose a levy, or tax, upon the trade of the merchants, giving the politicians a win, win situation, as they would fund

the annuity, through the tariff that they gathered. They calculated that the guaranteed return at six percent would cost them nothing, if not make them a profit.

The merchants—who one assumes were successful business men—figured that profits from trading in the New World and South America, would tide them over.

Within a matter of months, the value of stock in the merchant company soared. Apparently there would be no end to this rise in stock value. It could never end. This was mainly due to the Spanish, who were (it was rumoured) going to open up all of the ports in Chile and Peru and allow the merchants access to trade in untold amounts of precious commodities such as gold. Upon this speculation the future was set to be rosy. What could possibly go wrong?

In hindsight there was one small piece of news that was omitted from the headline. King Phillip V of Spain had let everyone involved know—including the merchants—that he was only going to allow a solitary merchant ship into one port, and one port only, once every year, and NOT one ship into each port, or even one ship into each colony. This lone ship would only be permitted to carry 500 tons of goods—including slaves, although the steep import duty in Britain upon slaves made this (abhorrent) trade unprofitable, therefore trade in precious commodities was essential to make the venture profitable. These small, but rather important details were held back from investors.

The very first ship set sail in 1717, six years post formation of the trading company. (It is surprising that many investors retained—and even added to—their investment even though no ship had sailed in six years!) The relations with Spain also soured. Further trading was nigh on impossible.

In no time at all—on paper—the company had made millions despite there being no inherent capital asset value within the merchant company. Many more companies were formed upon a similar basis. All were fuelled by similar speculation and rumour.

The directors of the South Sea Trading Company continued to maintain that further profits were just around the corner. In 1717 they had gained a further £2,000,000 of public debt. In 1719 they even achieved the astounding feat of outbidding the Bank of England for considerable amounts of government debt. This was eight years after founding the company. But still no significant levels of trade had come to fruition.

By 1719 the government's National Debt sat at a level of £18,300,000, of which £3,400,000 was held by the Bank of England, £3,200,00 by the British East India Company, and a staggering, £11,700,000 by the South Sea Trading Company! The remaining debt was in various forms of redeemable debt and long term annuities.

The directors of this trading company also came up with a great wheeze. They would sell shares to individuals—such as politicians and even the King's mistress—for nothing, with the promise of redeeming these shares, whenever the holder wished to do so, including the distribution of any profits on the share price. Put simply, people got shares for nothing, with the promise of high returns in the future, at a time of their own choosing. Many recipients of the free shares invested heavily into this gravy train.

In 1720 the British government gave even more credence to the whole operation by passing an act that is commonly called the: Bubble Act. This required all such new joint-stock companies to be incorporated. The share price of the trading company now leapt to a staggering £890 per share! This was an all time high from the initial £100 for each share at the formation of this company. This was also a return of over 100% for each and every year. In early August of 1720, the share price finally reached a staggering peak of £1,000 per share!

Would you have invested? For your investment you would have gained a guarantee at a rate of return between four percent to six percent; plus free shares; combined with the promise of untold wealth from unlimited trade overseas? (A question that has puzzled many who have studied the South Sea Bubble is why didn't those who were given shares, sell them when they had doubled, tripled or quadrupled?) Greed had supplanted common sense. You can imagine people sitting there, believing that they have an asset worth something, but what assets did the company own? Nothing at all. It owned a huge portion of the National Debt, but nothing else. As with all such schemes, the rot set in:

> The first instalment payments were due on the first and second money subscriptions of new stock in the company. Put simply, despite a devious scheme that had been devised earlier in the same year, the payments could not be met.
>
> In the September of 1720, the cries of: sell, sell, sell echoed around the city. The share price rapidly fell to £150 per share, from the all time high. Understandably, there were no buyers. The country now languished in poverty, holding enormous levels of National Debt. Many high profile figures in society were adversely affected; from politicians to the King's mistresses. Even the likes of Sir Isaac Newton and the composer Handel supposedly lost out.
>
> Some of the directors of the trading company fled the country, and those that stuck around to face the music were prosecuted. In 1721 a full investigation was launched and corruption was revealed—even within the cabinet. John Asiable, the Chancellor of the Exchequer was prosecuted along with other prominent cabinet members. Even a Lord or two did not miss out on judicial retribution. Asiable was imprisoned.
>
> The people who had been duped, their dreams of untold wealth had departed, literally in a bubble that had burst. At the time there were no state benefits to fall back on and many were literally ruined.

It is true that means of communication was far slower in the eighteenth century, and it is true that this was an isolated incident within the world, and today there is more connectivity and a global trade that was not in evidence at the time, and perhaps in the modern age such deceit would be hard to come by. But wait, who recalls the dot com bubble? Investors were pouring millions into the stock of companies within the technology sector. There was also the contract, sold by the U.K. Government for the next generation mobile phone. In 1999 investors poured into companies that were writing software and developing hardware to overcome the millennium bug. Our fridges were going to stop working, along with our microwave ovens, hoovers, dishwashers, washing machines etc… Business would be affected and lose millions as computer systems were going to crash. Emergency services would be stranded, hospitals would need to utilise generators as the national grid may stop working. Aeroplanes were in danger of falling from the sky. I recall all of these headlines, in the media, it was going to be catastrophic. (Whether anyone in the IT industry really believed this is another matter.) Some fund managers piled their clients money into companies that offered solutions to the problem. This was purely based upon speculation and rumour. There was no real capital value within these software and hardware development companies, they simply relied upon the fear of mankind that something was going to go wrong. We tried to overcome the apparent danger. I conclude that the folly of greed follows mankind around. History is full of examples of deviousness. Micah shows this is nothing new. Micah might be talking of housing and fields but he speaks out when people are being robbed of their livelihood. This is very different to the South Sea Bubble, but in both scenarios, at their heart, is man's desire for wealth and a situation whereby the upper echelon of society is corrupt.

Today we are living in the age of consequences, just as the people of Israel did. ***Turn your back on social justice, and calamity will overtake you***, Micah promises. Whether you believe in the divine or not, history backs up this proposition. I believe that there is the possibility of divine retribution, or at least a lack of divine intervention and protection, and this is the same as that which was revealed to Micah, who in turn spoke this message to the people of Israel. If God is a God of constants—as I believe he is—could the same happen to us, here and now?

In amongst all of this, whether it be the people of Israel, or the South Sea Bubble, or the dot com revolution that never was; at the very core lies the fallen sinful state of mankind. In history people have been prepared to cheat hard working farm owners out of their property; others have lied and cheated their way into gaining investors in order to inflate the share price of a dubious trading company; and many have followed the crowds by responding to unfounded fears that something might go wrong with their man-made technology.

What can we learn from all of this? Justice is essential to a society that claims to be civilised and today we are far away from true justice. For your own investments, remember the old adage that I cite again: if it looks too good to be true, then it is probably too good to be true. Remember also that wealth is transitory, in itself it is of no value or worth. Read these wise words from the book of Ecclesiastes, in the Holy Bible, that verifies the sentiment of my city friend Derek, regarding enough, never being enough:

> [10]Whoever loves money never has money enough;
> whoever loves wealth is never satisfied with his income.
> This too is meaningless.
> [11]As goods increase,
> so do those who consume them.
> And what benefit are they to the owner except to feast his eyes on them?...
> [15]Naked a man comes from his mother's womb,
> and as he comes, so he departs.
> He takes nothing from his labour that he can carry in his hand.

Alternatively, let's look to the book of Psalms, Chapter 49:

> [1]Hear this, all you peoples;
> listen, all who live in this world,
> [2]both low and high,
> rich and poor alike:...
> [10]For all can see that the wise die,
> that the foolish and the senseless also perish,

leaving their wealth to others.
¹¹Their tombs will remain their houses forever,
  their dwellings for endless generations,
  though they had named lands after themselves.
¹²Human beings, despite their wealth, do not endure;
  they are like the beasts that perish
¹³This is the fate of those who trust in themselves,
  and of their followers, who approve their sayings.
¹⁴They are like sheep and are destined to die;
  death will be their shepherd
  (but the upright will prevail over them in the morning).
  Their forms will decay in the grave…

CHAPTER SEVEN

CASH IS KING

Here is a story told to me by a friend of mine, let's call him John:

John is a vicar of a parish set in a typical country town in the county of Devon. Within his congregation is a bank manager who works for a well known high street bank.

In casual conversation the bank manager tells John that sometimes he finds his job hard. He is faced with a number of moral dilemmas that he cannot reconcile with his Christian faith. He tells John of two appointments, with two different clients during his previous week.

The first appointment is with a lady who wants to borrow £10,000 to have her boobs enlarged. She is good for the credit as she has passed the credit score with flying colours. The bank manager is obliged to grant the loan facility as she meets the criteria of his employer. She is a good risk for the loan. He has no choice and he approves the finance.

On the same day, the manager has an appointment with a livestock farmer. He has lost everything in the devastating foot and mouth outbreak (of a few years ago). He asks the bank manager for a short term loan of a measly £50. The farmer wants to buy enough food for his family, for just that week. The manager has to turn him down as he is a high risk client. The farmer has no means of repaying any loan, even one of fifty quid. In reality the bank does not lend such a small amount.

If you were the bank manager what would you have done? Please note that the rules of the bank state that you, as an employee, cannot personally lend, or give money to clients. If you do, then your own job is under threat.

In this story, the real value of £10,000 was worth far less than £50. Why? Because the lower amount could feed a family for a week. Most of us would perceive this as a far more essential need than breast enlargement surgery. The larger of these two loans would pay for a fancy surgeon; an anaesthetist; a nice bed in a private hospital; all in order to satisfy a person's desire for their perception of improvement and perfection. What is this compared to shopping in the supermarket in order to give your kids an evening meal? Perhaps the lady in question had some self esteem issues that needed addressing, this may have been her way of overcoming such issues. I don't know, but even so, cash to buy the basic commodity of food makes fifty quid of considerably greater value than ten grand in this situation.

Within society our concept of cash has become distorted. We might comment, as a friend did to me the other day, of a property developer:

He's well loaded.

My parents used to observe that:

He's not short of a bob or two.

But what is cash really worth? It is this sense of proportionality that I wish to put under the microscope in this chapter.

I wonder, if like me, you watch (rather too avidly in my case): The Apprentice. For those who do not watch this compelling top class programme, let me explain:

A dozen or more people compete for the chance to land a job, for just one year, on a salary of £100,000. In order to assess their potential, each week tasks are assigned by the entrepreneur Lord Alan Sugar. (There is also a version of this in the U.S. with Donald Trump as the wealthy businessman and task master). The tasks that are set each week are business orientated (to perceive that any of the tasks are, in reality, business orientated is stretching the point of reality to infinity). Each week the team who has made the most profit wins and they are given a treat. The losing team are given nothing. One of the contestants on the losing team gets "fired" by Lord Sugar in a board-room confrontation.

The way the contestants behave is saddening. I am left speechless at the vigour of the contestants—as they battle for survival—in the board-room when the time for eviction looms. Any form of friendship between them disappears. They fight and brawl—verbally at least—for survival. Then, post firing squad, the contestant who has been fired hugs the others who have just slagged them off! But why do they all want this job so much? Could it be that the job is seen as a short cut to riches by the contestants? (In the latest series being screened—autumn 2010—the cat fight between the losing girls team, in just the second week is simply staggering. I have never witnessed anything like this, in any business environment!)

I am also intrigued as to why the amount of personal wealth attributed to Lord Sugar is meant to mean anything. I assume that it is meant to impress, otherwise it would not be mentioned week in and week out in the programme's introduction, Lord Sugar is worth many millions we are informed. Amusingly there is no mention of Capital Gains Tax (CGT) that would need to be deducted from his wealth if he sold up.

Every so often we can check out the value of people, in monetary terms, on some form of rich list that the media publish from time to time. But why is this newsworthy? Why would we want to know how rich someone is? Does wealth really make one person more important than another? Is our identity so entrenched in how wealthy we all are?

Please note that I am not criticising any entrepreneur, Lord Sugar has made a stash load of money; he must employ quite a few people, which is good for the economy, but to identify and equate someone's worth, with their personal level of wealth, surely this is a misnomer.

How can we compare and value people, such as Lord Sugar, to the Macmillan nurse who cares for the sick and terminally ill? Can we really compare Lord Sugar, Sir Richard Branson, Bill Gates, Simon Cowell, David Beckham and co… to those who work amongst the homeless? What of the soldier on the front line, in battle, literally putting their lives on the line, for you and for me? What of the police officer, on the beat, confronting the mugger with a knife? What of the fire officer who plunges into a raging inferno without any thought for their own personal safety in order to rescue a child? What of the paramedic struggling to save the victim of a hit and run? What of the teacher trying to maintain discipline where gang violence is becoming increasingly common in their scholl? Has wealth, in our own minds, become so important that it overshadows us and how we see others? Does it now define us and how valuable we think we are to—and within—society? For example, a friend of mine said this once:

> When I went to a social function, in conversation people would inevitably ask me: What do you do?
>
> My reply would be: I am a teacher.
>
> They would normally ask me more about my job, until they eventually came to ask me: What age do you teach?
>
> My answer: I teach in a primary school.
>
> You could see them working this out, the cogs of their brain churning. She is reasonably bright, as she is a teacher, but she doesn't teach GCSE or A Levels, so she can't be that intelligent.

Strangers would label my friend's ability and they would class her level of intelligence according to her occupation. I can also guarantee that they have subconsciously assessed what her standard of living might be by guessing at her income. They assessed her worth by her job and her resulting remuneration.

We also judge each other by things like the car that we drive; the clothes we wear; where we live; where we go on vacation… so on and so forth. This outward display of wealth assists us in placing ourselves—and those that we meet—into a category of wealth and often their academic ability, or what we refer to as intelligence.

When we meet someone and once we have sussed out a person's job and the level of their wealth, we can then decide—perhaps subconsciously—should we be friends with them or not?

Children, when they meet, are very different in one regard, they just accept one another and interact with one another without such judgements. However they do have spats and these tend to revolve around things like the sharing of toys. But look at the value of some of the toys that they have argued over. I have seen toddlers contest over a small plastic ring when it has been snatched away by another kid! The material value of the bit of plastic is merely a few pence, but they argue nevertheless. It is this inherent protectionism of possessions that we tend to take into adulthood. As we grow older we begin to add on this tier of possessiveness a monetary value, and we want to accumulate stuff that has a value, rather than stuff itself. A whole marketing industry has grown up around this concept. The label and badge has become important. For example, the functionality of having a box on four wheels to transport us from reference point A to our destination at point B has diminished somewhat. What has become rather more important to us is the badge upon that box and all that the badge offers.

But is this desire for riches a new phenomena? Let's turn to my arbitrator and the book of James in the New Testament and Chapter 2:

> [1]My brothers, as believers in our glorious Lord Jesus Christ, don't show favouritism. [2]Suppose a man comes into your meeting wearing a gold ring and fine clothes, and a poor man in shabby clothes also comes in. [3]If you show special attention to the man wearing fine clothes and say, "Here's a good seat for you'" but say to the poor man, "You stand there" or "Sit on the floor by my feet," [4]have you not discriminated among yourselves and become judges with evil thoughts?

Just over two thousand years ago there was a problem in the early church. Favouritism was being shown. At the love feast called the Agape—that we now call Holy Communion—there was a tendency to honour the rich and disregard the poor. Here was a community that was meant to be founded upon love and equality for all, yet the richer you were, then you gained a greater level of respect and attention. The rich were also falling into the trap of displaying the trappings of their wealth and accepting the higher and more important seats at church services and meetings. They were lapping up this increased level of deference. It was a two way street.

I have tried to point out that the Holy Bible clearly shows that wealth is transitory. It is something that you cannot take with you, yet throughout history mankind has shown that we have an inherent switch that says give me money, stuff, and lots of it. Let's grab it, by fair means or by foul. Few have resisted it's lure. (I have just seen an interview with Mrs. Gates, wife of Bill, the founder of Microsoft. She has stated that they wish to give away 95% of their wealth, in their lifetime to good causes of health and education. Fantastic I say, but I wonder how much the 5% that is left is worth? But hey, who am I to criticise? As I have pointed out at the very start of this book, I am rich beyond measure when compared to farmers in the sub-continent. Furthermore, we must not judge one another.)

A demonstration of this continuing lust can be found within the fictional tale of the one ring in the Tolkein trilogy: Lord of the Rings. In this book, a ring of power has been found. People have fought over the ring, they have even killed for it. It has a lure that few can resist. The creature Gollum has been transformed into a disfigured, contorted and ugly figure, over many years, as a consequence of his holding onto the ring of power for some considerable amount of time. During this time of possession he has hidden away from the world, shielding the ring from any who wanted to take it from him. He wants to possess this ring of power for possessions sake. As soon as he found it, he fought and killed his friend to hold onto it. He did nothing with the ring, apart from retention in this perverse form of possession. In his solitude his point of reference in valuing what was important revolved around the one ring. In this tale we can see what such a lust for possession can do, even though it is just a story it is a good analogy.

In the infamous tale: A Christmas Carol, by Charles Dickens, the main character of this story, Ebeneezer Scrooge, has become embittered and twisted. He only cares for his wealth that he has hoarded and hidden away from the world. He is devoid of compassion for others. He does not wish to take part in celebration and jollity. Wealth for wealth's sake has become his plumb line. It is only when he is visited by Spirits and he is forced to confront his past, present and future, that he begins to care for others. When faced with mortality and his mistakes, and a dour future, he sets about reparation. Finally he realises the value of wealth. He can become profligate. I wonder if the Bankers and financiers of today can face the mistakes of their past and begin to relinquish their own wealth and rewrite their own obituaries?

In the Holy Bible, Yeshua (Jesus) talks of true wealth. These are his words in the book of Matthew, Chapter 13:

> [45]"Again, the kingdom of heaven is like a merchant looking for fine pearls. [46]When he found one of great value, he went away and sold everything he had and bought it."

This is amazing. The kingdom of heaven and all that it offers is worth more than anything we own. It is worth selling everything, our houses, cars, video games, computers, mobile phones, literally everything, in order to gain the kingdom of God. This does not mean that the kingdom of heaven can be bought, it is just an analogy. It speaks of our possessions as being worthless when compared to this kingdom. We need to learn this. But let me ask this: how hard would it be to sell all that you own?

Essentially stuff and money is worthless, but we have placed an inflated value upon it all. We have come to identify what someone is worth by the amount of cash that is in their bank. Sadly, this went on in the Christian church two thousand years ago, and I have seen it happen, in the church of today. For example, I recall one vicar saying to me, of a wealthy city accountant who was a member of their congregation:

> I have seen them flash the cash.

If the city worker wanted something to be done in the church they would say, or imply to the staff team, if you do this thing, then I will give you money for the other thing that you so desperately want. They were prepared to lay down the option of subtle monetary persuasion, just to get their own way! What is sad about this story, is that three Revs—who worked in this church at different times—said the exact same thing, about this individual in this church over a number of years.

There is also a tendency to want wealth without hard work. Just look at the length of the queues at the auditions for reality shows such as: X-Factor; Britain's Got Talent (BGT); etc... There is a desire for dreams to be fulfilled, for fortunes to be made. For many it is seen as the only route to any form of fulfilment. I know a few musicians and bands who tour pubs and clubs performing to crowds—to use the word crowds is perhaps an exaggeration—of between a dozen to a couple of hundred at most. It takes hard graft to make it in any sphere, but we live in a society with fast food; fast paced TV programmes; fast lifestyles—the washing machine, dishwasher, hoover, microwave etc… all of which were meant to give us more leisure time (this is proven to be an utter myth), and we are no happier today than we ever were.

On the aforementioned talent show of BGT, what happens when a 12 year old kid gets their hopes dashed and they get voted off? Often they are devastated to have their dream come to an abrupt end, their identity is so wrapped up in their perception of their own talent. Post rejection during a live interview, it is the most important day of their life, they sob. No it isn't I want to scream! You haven't even begun to live! You have a lifetime ahead of you. Buckle down and enjoy what lies ahead. What about getting a degree/apprenticeship; getting married; having kids; experiencing divorce; bereavement; being declared clear of cancer after a course of chemotherapy etc…all of these are pretty important life experiences, and that kid off the talent show may not go through all of these life experiences, indeed one would not wish them to do so, but at 12 years of age, or even at 20 or 30, your life (in the West at least) has only just begun. The rejected contestants will have far more important days ahead of them than performing in front of three or four judges who may, or may not know, what they are talking about. But they cannot see it. They want their dream to be fulfilled, immediately, here and now, or at least within a period of twelve weeks or so—that is by the conclusion of the current series—for this is their expectation. It is seen almost as being their right that they gain that lucrative contract.

In the current series of the X-Factor, there is the alleged scandal of auditionees having their vocal talents being manipulated by something called auto-tuning. Editing of the auditions apparently shows some contestants more in tune than they really are. Cries of foul and cheat resound. But why are viewers so surprised? There is nothing real about these shows. They are divorced from reality. They are simply made into good telly to make money, nothing more, nothing less. Just like the Bankers, profits are the bottom line. You are mistaken to think otherwise. (I know someone who went through the initial stages of the auditions of the X-Factor. It takes two or three days to get in front of the judges and people who are terrible are picked by producers of the show over the many with considerable talent. The final few selected by producers appear in front of judges for the sake of good TV. Why on earth does anyone think that it is any different than this?)

It cannot be denied that stars have been born from these talent shows, such as: Leona Lewis; Susan Boyle; JLS; Diversity and so on, and I wish them all well, but this pursuit of a dream to wealth and riches is puzzling. We were created to worship a living God, not money and possessions! This hunger for the shortcut, the quick route to fortune, that can rise up within all of us, to a greater or lesser degree. It is—I believe—this perversion of the very created order of God and our stepping away from the divine that is largely the reason for the economic crisis facing our world today. This same hunger for riches on talent shows is evident in the financial markets.

So is cash really worth anything? Let's take this question further. Imagine that a cool one million pounds is stacked up right in front of you, here and now. Put a value upon this physical stack of dormant cash in front of you. Does it have an intrinsic value, apart from the paper and ink? I would contest that this money is completely worthless. Having £1,000,000 on you now, or in your bank account is just a digit in your mind, then poof, it's gone. A paper balance on a bank account is meaningless, utterly meaningless, it is what that money could buy if you used it that gives cash a value.

Have you ever come across the following parable, told by Yeshua (Jesus). It is recorded in the Holy Bible in the book of Luke and Chapter 12:

> [16]And he told them this parable: "The ground of a certain rich man produced good crop. [17]He thought to himself, 'What shall I do? I have no place to store my crops?'
>
> [18]"Then he said, 'This is what I'll do. I will tear down my barns and build

> bigger ones, and there I will store all my grain and my goods. [19]And I'll say… "take life easy,…"'
> [20]But God said to him, 'You fool! This very night your life will be demanded from you. Then who will get what you have prepared for yourself?'
> [21]"This is how it will be with anyone who stores up things for himself but is not rich toward God."

A few points on these verses. Do you recall the verses of scripture that say enough, never appears to be enough. This parable starts with this bloke already being rich. He already has more than enough. He then has a bumper crop, and what does he do? Does he give to the poor and needy out of his abundance? No, he wants to store the perishable crops for himself. He is the epitomy of Scrooge. But how will he ever use it all? There is only so much in the way of Cornflakes or Weetabix that any one person can eat! He has plenty yet he gives nothing. The teaching is this (and this is a recurring theme in the Holy Bible): wealth is transitory, in the grand scheme of things, all wealth is worthless. But the attitude of this farmer results in an experience of a false reward here and now. All wealth stays on the earth; that is the best that you can get, there's nothing else left we are told. The end point to wealth is finite as we will all die, one day! But, there is hope. God's riches hold out for a greater potential and worth. His riches are well beyond the world that we see and live within. God's riches are not transitory, they are solid, and firm. Hunger after God's grace, his richness and his goodness, you will then have inherited something of value, we are instructed. Anything else pales in comparison.

Whether you believe in divine intervention or not, the reality is—as I have said—you cannot take it with you. Yeshua (Jesus) precedes the telling of this story with the following words:

> [15]…"Watch out! Be on your guard against all kinds of greed; a man's life does not consist in the abundance of his possessions."

Our identity should not be tied up in how much money we have in our bank; nor is it about how much stuff we own, or the car that we drive. For the Christian the level of our wealth should be meaningless to both ourselves and those in fellowship around us. The church should be setting an example to the world in these matters, sadly many of us Christians fall short, me included!

You may be wondering why, in a book on the global banking crisis am I going down this repetitious cul-de-sac? Hopefully all will now become clearer.

Our society is engaging in this desire and hunger for defining cash and our concept of worth. We are even defining this in the manner that we invest, and why we invest. Many of us view investments in monetary terms, we might ask of our advisers and fund managers:

> …have my investments made money or lost money over the last: day; week; month; quarter or year?

My colleague in the city, Derek, agreed on this point when he said the following:

> The trading desks in the city are interesting. Their sole job is to make money, and not necessarily acquire capital value. They invest in order to gain a percentage return. That's not me, or my game. I want to invest my clients money to increase the capital asset value of their portfolio.

Do you recall the South Sea Bubble that I referred to in the previous chapter. Investors were investing money based upon pure speculation, into a company that held nothing of any value. Today a similar investment might be technology based, such as a mobile phone service provider, or an Internet Service Provider (ISP). Just like the South Sea Bubble and the resulting fiasco, we must ask what do these companies own? In the manner of assets that have a capital value, they own very little. They might have a client bank of people who subscribe to their services, but those clients could just as easily go elsewhere. For example, the clients could jump ship when a newer and better service provider comes along offering a cheaper service? These types of companies might continue to make a profits, year on year—I am not saying do not invest into these companies—but the level of their profits do have a ceiling as there will only be a maximum number of subscribers to the services offered by such companies. In order to increase profits they must bring in newer technology and convince us to buy more stuff, or upgrade to a faster internet based service, or they must acquire other companies in order to extend the number of clients who are using their services. And so, the huge conglomerates will grow. We are happy with the subsequent growth, as our pensions, savings and investments increase in value with this global expansion and domination, until monopolies are formed as this often results in less choice and less competition. This can result in higher prices, or even price fixing within a certain sector by the few.

A recent example of a large company going from being asset rich, to asset poor, and the effect that this had upon their cash flow, is the store Woolworths. These problems were diagnosed by many analysts including Elizabeth Rigby the Consumer Industries Editor of the Financial Times, in her article in November 2008. In this article she reported as follows:

> This week the fight to save the much-loved but very under-shopped Woolworths chain finally drew to a close as the 800 stores and the wholesale distribution arm were placed into administration.
>
> Having limped along for seven years, with the profit line gradually shifting from black to red, the directors finally called it a day after the retailer, labouring under £385 million ($591 million) of debt, succumbed to a cash crisis.
>
> But how did it come to pass that the near 100-year-old chain, which in its heyday was opening a store a week and was still selling £1.7 billion of goods a year through its stores at the time of its collapse, should end up in such a dire predicament?…
>
> "It was already not a very strong format and it was suddenly coming under more competitive pressure and it didn't have the safety valve of being backed by property," says Mr. Shiret [an analyst at Credit Suisse].
>
> By last summer, the rot had become so bad that Geoff Ruddell, analyst at Morgan Stanley, warned that the retail business was worthless…
>
> This week, Woolworths' fans were blaming its bankers for the variety chain

store's demise. But while the credit crunch has proved the final catalyst, the seeds of Woolworths failure were sown many years before.

When the company hit troubled times, instead of restructuring their business model they tapped into the asset. They sold off their real estate, which plugged the deficit gap for a few years, but they had to start paying rent on property that they had previously owned.

When they hit very stormy waters once more, and when trading was in decline, the increased overheads of rental could not be met. As a company they had nothing more to sell, apart from their stock in a closing down sale.

This is just one example where the collection of people called Bankers have been blamed for the demise of something that is not their fault. It is so easy to point the accusing finger at these so called Bankers and to blame them whilst they are under fire from the media. They are an easy target. In the case of Woolworths nothing could be further from the truth. Primarily, due to increasing rents, combined with a failure to adapt, like the dinosaurs, the store finally died out. Woolworths had no capital asset value, such as property, to fall back on. They held large volumes of outdated stock that no one wanted to buy. They did not move with the times.

The U.K. government have adopted a similar policy of being outdated. They have no assets of real value left, as everything has been sold off. They are now left with nothing of value. Instead of adapting and restructuring the National Debt by cutting back on spending some years ago, they have literally sold off the family silver, or in this case the nation's gold reserves, at a knock down price. This plugged the deficit gap for a while, but the nation has hit stormy waters once again. Now there are no reserves to fall back on. The vaults of the Bank of England are full of gold that is not ours. (Over the next ten to fifteen years, some very difficult economic and spending decisions are going to have to be made, no matter which political colour might be in power.)

As investors what happens to us when we hit a similar personal maelstrom. Do we have capital assets to fall back upon, on deposit, within the clearing banks? And what of our investments. Most of us want our investment portfolios to continually grow, we want the upside, but no downside. A freelance compliance officer—who works within the financial services sector—recently told me the following story about a visit that he made to an office of a financial advisory firm:

> Around twenty advisers were at their desks. All of the advisers, except one, were fielding calls, from concerned clients, about their investments that were falling in value, like a stone. I asked the one adviser why he was not having to take any calls from his clients. He said, 'I have asked my clients not to ring me unless their investments fall in value, in a short period of time, by more than 30%. As a result, I don't get any calls from worried clients when there is a fall in the markets.'

That solitary adviser had been brave, but wise. He had given his clients a clear measurement of risk and reward, when his clients invested. My friend in the city, Derek, says this:

> Clients will ring me if their investments fall by 15%, or 20%, but they never ring me when their investments have gone up by the same percentage.

This is true. During the good times no one really complains about growth rates; or the potential losses; the lending policies of Bankers; the bonus culture of Bankers; the excesses of Bankers; etc... Generally speaking everyone is happy to see their investment portfolios, property and pensions apparently increasing in value, but this is often only based upon growth in the short term and an annual statement that shows a cash figure higher than the previous year. But as we have learned, cash is worth nothing, in itself. I recently heard the following, from a well known investment house that should know better. Someone from this popular, and well known, company's trading desk said:

> We have moved our position from holding a large proportion of equities, instead we now invest up to 15% to 20% into cash, because we don't want to lose our shirts, quite frankly.

This short term approach to investment continues to shock me. What this trader was saying, in simple terms—on certain investment funds—they had decided to shore up against losses. They had made gains in the past, but they were extremely worried about the double dip that currently gets a lot of air time. They had opted to batten down the hatches until the worst is over. This is fine and dandy, but it is the last part of this statement that disturbs me. I have been working in the financial services sector for nigh on twenty years, and I continually hear this phrase (or a phrase like it):

> We don't want to lose *our* shirts.

I'm sorry, is it your money that you are investing and risking, Mr. Fund Manager? My own mentor, a wise adviser named Peter Took, when I started out in financial services, said this to me:

> Don't ever think that it is your money that you are dealing with, once you do that, you have lost your integrity. It is your client's money, and it should always been seen as such.

The vast majority of Independent Financial Advisers (IFAs) who run their own businesses adhere to this sensible mantra. But I once heard the following from a tied financial adviser many years ago:

> Once, I went to see a client, with my manager, and we convinced them to take out an endowment savings plan, by telling the client it was just like a Christmas savings club scheme. The adviser laughed, uproariously.

Or how about this somewhat worse tale which was related to me by a friend who also worked as a tied agent. This was many moons ago. Let's call my friend Michael:

> Michael had just started working as a financial adviser for a large institution. He was undergoing some training. As part of this training he was required to carry out some accompanied visits to potential clients with his manager. On this particular visit his manager said that he would show him how to conduct

an interview.

The interview was conducted, with Mr. and Mrs. Jones, in their house, while the two children sat in the corner reading and playing quietly. Eventually the children were asked to go upstairs to change for bed by their parents. Dutifully they did so.

The manager continued with the interview. He explained to Mr. and Mrs. Jones that life cover was a good idea. They said that they would like to think about it. The children came back downstairs to say good night to their parents.

The children hugged their mum and dad, said good night to Michael, and his manager. This is where it all…well I will let you decide what to think of what happened next.

The manager stepped in and he addressed the two kids. 'Before you go to bed, I would like to tell you something,' they all paused, wondering just what he could have to say to the two obedient offspring of Mr. and Mrs. Jones. The manager then continued. 'Do you know that your mummy and daddy don't love you.'

The children looked crestfallen. Michael could not quite believe it. With their lip quivering, and choking back the tears, the son asked, 'What do you mean mummy and daddy don't love us?'

The manager looked them straight in the eye and said: 'Well, if they die there will not be enough money for both of you, so no-one will be able to look after you.'

The children burst into tears. The son implored of his parents, 'You're not going to die are you?'

Let me give you a moment to consider this scenario. Have you recovered? Let's continue.

Thankfully these stories are from a long time ago and regulation has more or less put a stop to this type of practice, but I have heard and seen it all. I have seen advisers forge client signatures on documents. I know that in one firm they held an adviser amnesty upon forged client signatures on application forms. Declare any forgeries—advisers were informed—then you will be O.K. One firm eventually sacked one of their top performing advisers, knowing full well that he had forged client signatures. The CEO of that company oversaw this sacking and offered favourable terms to the sacked adviser! I heard of some advisers, in various firms, running what are called Ponzi schemes for large financial institutions (more on Ponzi in a while). This practice was carried on in full view of other advisers and their managers. No-one batted an eyelid because the legal business being gained by the advisers was so profitable that they all turned a blind eye to this illegal practice.

It must be said that the whole financial services industry has improved markedly since. This is a good thing. It gives me hope that change can be bought about—and in around twenty years I have met many more good and decent advisers than bad and corrupt ones—but the changes that regulation have bought about are imposed, they have not been voluntary. It is not down to the human heart that such malpractice has become virtually non-existant, it is down to an imposition of rules and regulations that have come about through public outrage.

I cannot, hand on heart, say how all traders—and advisers—view investment monies, I do not know them well enough to comment, but when the sales teams of fund managers and investment houses run seminars and make such statements that allude to this losing of one's shirt, I suspect that this might be a fair reflection of attitudes that exist upon the trading floor today.

I look forward to the day when the mind set of the city is not focussed upon how much can I make on this for me through making quick returns to increase my bonus. Rather the attitude should be how can I increase the overall asset value of my clients portfolios, in the longer term. For this I look to the likes of my friend Derek, and others like my mentor, Peter Took.

I would like to interject at this point that some of what has gone on is no more than we deserve. Collectively we have looked for an ever increasing return on our investments—few who invest, whether this be in stock markets, property, vintage cars or wine, ever expect their investments to decrease by 30% or more in a relatively short period of time. We have lost sight of the fact that there is always the possibility of losing money in any investment, even when fund managers and advisers are doing a good job. We must come to realise that the value of our portfolios can, one day, be like the South Sea Trading Company, worthless. This can be what a recession—or depression—can bring about. Currently I am worried about the sharp growth in the markets of the past few months. Investors are now returning to the markets on the back of this short term growth. Many have not learned the lessons of the past. Invest yes, as I think that there is evidence that equities is a good place to be right now, but do so on the understanding that nothing is certain and with caution.

If we acknowledge that cash is inherently worthless, their wealth is transitory, and if we are stewards of all that we have, and if we maintain a belief that worldly wealth is indeed worthless, the losses that we will inevitably experience will be far easier to bear. (Personally I am not at this stage yet and I am not being flippant about the advice process that I undertake with my clients, I will always try to do the best for my clients.) I believe—or at least I try to believe—that all I have is God's and not mine. I do not really own anything. This is what Yeshua (Jesus) said, following the parable that I cited earlier:

> [22]…"Therefore I tell you, do not worry about your life, what you will eat; or about your body, what you will wear. [23]Life is more than food, and the body more than clothes. [24]Consider the ravens: They do not sow or reap, they have no storeroom or barn, yet god feeds them. And how much more valuable you are than birds! [25]Who of you by worrying can add a single hour to his life? [26]Since you cannot do this very little thing, why do you worry about the rest? [27]Consider how the lilies grow. They do not labour or spin. Yet I tell you not even Solomon in all his splendour was dressed like one of these. [28]If that is how God clothes the grass of the field, which is here today, and tomorrow is thrown into the fire, how much more will he clothe you,…[29]And do not set your heart on what you will eat or drink; do not worry about it.

Of course this is hard to achieve. For me not to worry is utterly alien. But life, we are told, is more than food; the body is more than clothes! Amazing teaching. Without faith, this teaching is nigh on impossible to accept, but with faith and by the power of the Holy Spirit, we have a fighting chance to change our fallen broken hearts and we can begin to move away from hanging onto transitory wealth and the stuff that litters our lives.

I reiterate that we should not operate as stewards who do not care, that is not what my arbitrator, says, we should try to be good stewards in all that we have, but we are stewards nothing more, nothing less. The role of the adviser is to assist clients in this role of stewardship. I believe that the wealth and riches that we have access to is due to the generosity of our God in heaven.

Much of what I say is from a position of relative comfort. It must be very hard to acknowledge this concept of stewardship if you are a single parent living on a sink estate with major financial worries and concerns accompanying such an existence; or when someone becomes incapacitated and unable to work, the bills just pile up, unpaid; or when someone is made redundant there appears to be little to no hope of gaining a new job when you are in your fifties (or older) as firms only want to recruit younger people. This is where social justice should step in giving hope to those with little hope. At the point of poverty, no matter what has caused the situation of poverty, the likes of Credit Action and CAP (Christians Against Poverty) and their free delivery of debt counselling guidance and advice must enter into the frame. This must also be combined with the provision of an essential state based benefit system.

Our society that has demanded—and continues to demand—the immediacy of ownership of possessions, a desire to have cash worth, has all contributed to the banking and credit crisis. Together, fund manager and investor alike, we wanted a rapid growth in our investments—which was unrealistic—without much thought or understanding for the consequences of a downturn. When it goes wrong we, the investors, want to have someone to blame other than ourselves. Of course the city is not blameless, they must shoulder some of the responsibility, as should the politicians, but the current crisis cannot be laid solely on the doorstep of the group that have become known as Bankers.

Let's return to the story of the South Sea Trading Company, just briefly. Post crash of this company a restructuring occurred and the share price settled at £150 each share. Consider this for a moment. The share price at the establishment of the company was the standard £100. This means—taking the final share price of £150 per share at the time of the company's collapse—there had been a realistic increase in the share price over a period of nine years, of 50%. This averages out at over 5% per annum. Today this would be seen as a healthy level of return. In the many bubbles of the past, greed drove speculation towards corruption and the desire to achieve vastly unrealistic returns. Corruption may not be as rife today as it was over two or three centuries ago, but the hunger within us to gain short term returns, with resulting wealth—even though this is a figure on a piece of paper—does not appear to have diminished. Until we hold onto the realism of accepting gains and losses in equal measure, the potential for this turmoil remains.

Rather than placing our trust in a figure on a computer print out, there is another way, a route that holds out a far greater reward, it is a greater hope. The divine offers us a greater investment return than we could ever desire or imagine.

In the conclusion of this chapter—and returning to where we started—let's move away from assessing one another by what we earn, the cars we drive and the clothes that we wear. We are equal in the eyes of God, and we are all loved by God in equal measure, even those we have labelled as Bankers. If you ever have the privilege to meet Lord Alan Sugar, or Bill Gates, approach them both as your equal, yes treat them with due deference and respect, just as you should treat anyone else that you might happen to meet whilst you are living on this, God's own earth. If you should ever be lucky enough to appear on the X-Factor or any other talent show, please do not place any great store by it or by any adulation that you may receive. If you win that record deal, please be a good steward and acknowledge the generosity of God.

Once we have these issues of expectation, equality, ownership and stewardship sorted out, surely the world will be a far better place to live in as our hearts and our minds will be transformed. We need to rediscover this "understanding" that we will perish, and that our wealth and "splendour" will remain here on earth. Admiring the prosperous is one thing, but to praise someone and hold them up as being better than another person, just because they are rich, that is very far from the created order of God. When we stand before the gates of heaven, what we have earned and owned will be entirely worthless. How we have praised the rich and influential, will also be worthless. It is our hearts that will be examined. How closely aligned to the heart of God, was our own heart will be the ultimate test? This fact will be exposed for all to see.

We need to allow those in the city to make mistakes. They should not have to work under an assumed expectation of only give me growth, with no downside. This shifting of our aspirations will make us far more resilient to the vagaries of any future crisis if we mange to obtain—and live by—these ideals. Then we will surely begin to reflect some of the heavenly principles and values as the condition of the heart changes and begins to transform from a blame and greed culture.

This is about moving our eyes from looking downwards and at one another, to looking upwards, away from the wealth of this world, to the wealth that our creator God offers to us. Matters began to go awry in the world, when man focussed upon what they did not have and mankind lost sight of God's commands that were in place for our protection. It is this inherited view that needs to be moved, quite radically, to a reliance upon God's generous provision, and a re-learning of the commands that were—and indeed remain—in place. This is an essential foundation that has been lost and needs to be re-discovered, by all of us. Without such a level of discovery our financial capitals will remain unchanged and there will be little hope for any form of transformation of our hearts, for as this unknown person once said:

It takes hands to build a house, but only hearts can build a home.

Are our hands so intent upon building up material wealth that our hearts are failing to build a true home? Are our hearts are now so far away from the home of our heavenly father? I earnestly believe that we are being called home. We have a call to partake in a dwelling place that God offers. Paul refers to the power that emanates from this home as a reality when writing to his protégé, Timothy. In Chapter 1 of Paul's second letter to the young man, whom Paul regards as his son, he writes that Timothy has at his disposal not:

[7]...a spirit of timidity, but a spirit of power, of love and of self-discipline.

We too have this same power available. We only have to ask for guidance in this turbulent times from this supernatural power that we call Ruach, or the very breath of God.

Whether we have faith; no faith; little faith; or an abundance of faith; many of us like the concept of security being entrenched in a power of the miraculous. This may bring comfort to us as we like to perceive a God of love and the supernatural. We also like to think that people love us and accept us for who we are. But to think that we have a God who wants us to be disciplined, and what is more, that he desires for us to accept this discipline and we are to become disciplined in our lives, we find this discomforting. This teaching points to a life that is considered and thought through, but a life that has constraints attaching to it. This is a far cry from a totally free market and a life of do anything you want, as long as it does not hurt anyone.

Let's aspire to re-learn the commands of God; let's re-discover what it is to dwell and bask in the resounding love of God and under his discipline. Let's test out what it is to live by faith and in his power and under his resolve; then our riches will fall away, they will become insignificant to us once we see the insurmountable riches that are on offer to us. Once we have this perception then the bonus culture of Bankers; the apparent importance of the wealth of multi-millionaires; our jealousy, greed and avarice; will all disappear.

Yes, we can respect and admire—as I have said—entrepreneurs, but we need to treat one another as equals in our dealings with one another, rich and poor alike. We cannot do this alone. The hearts of mankind and the beating heart of the financial markets will not be transformed without divine intervention and discipline.

Where does your heart lie? Let's examine this a little more, in the following chapter, commencing with a story about myself, and my own pride and arrogance.

CHAPTER EIGHT

HOW MUCH!

As outlined in the previous chapter our classification of a persons worth, according to their wealth, is on display in most parts of society whether it be at the local golf, rowing or yacht club; or in the work place when looking at the line of BMs and Mercs in the office car park. It has become a badge of honour to display the trappings of our riches.

In the media every day there is an incessant feed that wealth is good—unless you are in the receipt of Bankers' bonuses—and in almost every strata of society that I can think of, you are deemed to be successful if you are wealthy. This is the case in most cultures I should imagine. It is just that the means in which we might assess and display wealth that will differ between the various cultures. For example, I am quite portly and within the culture of the region that I visit in Kenya I am considered to be wealthy. The residents of this area know nothing of my own personal circumstances, but visually, to them, being plump is a symbol of wealth. This has probably come about because food is in short supply in the region and it is expensive. The thought process is that if someone has an inch or two excess around their mid region, they must be wealthy in order to be able to afford so much food.

I can recall a small event in my own life when I wanted to impress a friend of mine. The sad tale is as follows:

> I was a member of a local Gym, it was quite a reasonable set up. I was in the bar post workout with a friend of mine. I took out my wallet to pay for the round of drinks. Ever so proudly I withdrew my brand new sparkling Platinum American Express card. I believed that this would impress my friend who was standing next to me.
>
> The Amex card was taken from me by the bar staff. I took the opportunity to explain to my friend—with some considerable pride—as to why I had applied for this additional debit card.
>
> Mid pride, the barman returned to say that the debit transaction had failed

on my brand new card. He was sorry, he explained, but they did not accept Amex!

In this situation my own so very flashy Platinum Card was worthless as it was unacceptable. It was very embarrassing. I wanted the floor to swallow me up.

Sadly, this desire to display wealth as a symbol of our success has crept into all aspects of our lives. The church does not always escape this temptation. In some parts of the early church this was also very much the case. This is nothing new. I recall seeing the following take place, during a service that I attended:

A collection was being taken to raise funds to enable the youth group to purchase an electronic keyboard for their worship meetings. A basket was held up at the front of the church by the youth leader. The wealthiest were encouraged to go first, they had to place their large offerings into the basket. If the donation was of a sufficiently large amount they were asked to speak into a microphone, tell the congregation how much they were giving and why. This public display was carried out in order to encourage others to give. (I call it shaming others into giving.)

Gradually, the amount of each gift lessened in value. Those who put in lesser amounts were not given the opportunity to speak.

After a while—and as the gifts had decreased in value—a smartly dressed member of the youth came forward to give her offering. Discreetly she placed a wad of notes, in amongst the smaller gifts. She went to make her way back to her seat. The leader, who was holding the basket happened to see the fistful of notes that this lady had placed quietly into the basket. She was summoned back by the leader with a loud shout, the leader took out of the basket the donation and he held up the wad of notes that this young lady had given high in the air, for all to see. The young lady was asked to speak into the microphone. Almost in a whisper, she explained why she was making the donation. She scurried away and sat down as soon as she was allowed to do so.

I felt for this young lady. Clearly, she had tried her hardest to make the donation unseen. She had waited until the donation levels had dropped, wanting to affiliate herself with the lower level of giving in an attempt to make her gift discretely. The culture of the church had fallen into the trap of defining the value of giving by the size of the gift. Wealth was more important than the act of giving. The identity of people's worth, at that moment, in that church, was valued by how much they could give. Giving did not only relate to the willingness of the heart. There was no reference point to sacrificial giving, judgement had come into the sacrament of giving. No doubt people who gave the least felt shamed. Let's refer to some teaching of Yeshua (Jesus), in the book of Mark and Chapter 12:

> [41]Jesus sat down opposite the place where the offerings were put and watched the crowd putting their money into the temple treasury. Many rich people threw in large amounts. [42]But a poor widow came and put in two very small copper coins, worth only a fraction of a penny. [43]Calling his disciples to him, Jesus said, "I tell you the truth, this poor widow has put more into the treasury than all the others. [44]They all gave out of their wealth, but she, out of her poverty, put in everything—all she had to live on."

There are several things to note here. Firstly, the rich people are giving in abundance and not sacrificially. But more than this, look how they are giving. They are throwing in the coins. Their loud declarations of praise and thanksgiving that spewed out of their mouths are a means of getting people to look at their piety. Their actions are saying look at me, look at how much I give, this is how wealthy I am. Within this dramatic display of their wealth lies their identity. They are so full of arrogance and importance that the act of giving excessive amounts of money in front of the crowds has become their primary objective and the act of giving has been defiled. Imagine the loud chink of the coins as they threw in one coin after another; or, perhaps they tipped them in, the coins resounding loudly. I also guarantee that these gifts were made at the busiest times, at the height of the various festivals in Jerusalem when pilgrims from throughout the known world were present. Yeshua (Jesus) knew that this quiet woman had given up everything. Her gift was of a higher value than the total amount given by all of the wealthy. The woman had been called over by the Rabbi Yeshua (Jesus), for he used the words: "this poor widow"; and not: "that widow over there", but "this poor widow". This is another encounter with the one that we call Jesus. It was a dramatic teaching encounter for his disciples.

There is something extremely profound in this story. The wealthy were giving to the work of God and to the poor and here was one of the poor. She was meant to be a recipient of the wealth that was being given by the wealthy, for these gifts were meant to bring relief to the poor, yet she has probably received nothing. The system was corrupt. The wealthy got wealthier, the poor remained poor. The teaching is so challenging. There is a distinct shaming of the wealthy, their arrogance is condemned. It is evident that the gifts that they pour into the temple treasury are failing—in such a shameful manner—to reach those who needed it the most. But even when this nameless woman had little, to no chance, of receiving anything from this display of abundance, she still gave. I find this astounding, she gave money to the temple of God out of faithfulness, knowing that her offering was everything she owned. She must have been aware that the benefit system at the time was utterly corrupt. Despite all of this, she gives!

The wonderful teacher, Yeshua (Jesus), said to the disciples that "this woman" has given more than all those who are pouring in many thousands into the treasury. She gave a fraction of a penny. The tiny chink it made as it fell into the pot would have been no sound on earth at all. Yet in heaven the chink of that small coin resounded as loud as the loudest of a crashing cymbal. The host of the heavens must have stood still. They would have been astounded at this act, an act that must have appeared so very small in the eyes of mankind, if it was seen at all. This anonymous widow of history is a stark and clear demonstration of humility and faithfulness in action.

We can understand this encounter by delving even deeper into the teaching of this Rabbi. Looking in the book of Matthew and Chapter 6 we can read:

> [2]So when you give to the needy, do not announce it with trumpets as the hypocrites do in the synagogues and on the streets, to be honoured by men I

tell you the truth, they have received their reward in full. ³But when you give to the needy, do not let your left hand know what your right hand is doing, ⁴so that your giving may be in secret. Then your Father, who sees what is done in secret, will reward you.

This teaching is quite dramatically black and white (perhaps that is why I love it—I can be rather all or nothing in my nature). Give, and give whatever you want, but do it quietly, in secret, don't make a big thing of it. If you are motivated into giving, then give silently, just as this widow did, for your gift and the amount of the gift is between you and God and it should remain so.

This is something that we find hard in society. For example, do you watch the likes of: Children in Need; Comic Relief etc… Firstly I must emphasise that the money raised in these shows is phenomenal and I am not knocking these efforts and those of the participants in these shows. But my question is simple. Why does it take so many celebrities, comedians, pop stars and so on, to motivate us to give? Think for a moment of the amount of publicity that all of the high street brands gain from the prime time TV exposure on these shows. This publicity is due to the fund raising efforts of their own employees. The motivation of the employees may be well meaning, but does this same philanthropic attitude emanate from the directors and board members of these same companies, it is free advertising after all? Am I being too cynical?

Give in secret, we are commanded. Don't make a big show of it, even when giving to the needy. The founder of Microsoft and his wife have announced that they are to give the majority of their wealth to various good causes. In itself this might be good and healthy, but they have also said that they wish to get others to do the same. I would agree that Mr. and Mrs. Bill Gates do not appear to be making this gift with similar motives as those in the temple courts of over two thousand years ago, but it could be taken that they are implying that they are in judgement over the rich. It could be taken that the Gates are declaring:

We are the role model. We have the patent on what is right and proper in regard to giving. If you copy us then you are with us and the programme, you are then as good as we are. If you decide not to give as generously, then you are not with us.

This may not be their motive at all, but they are treading on dangerous ground as it could be interpreted as such. I know of wealthy people who do support good causes, quite silently, behind the scenes. I firmly believe that my arbitrator states that giving is best, when it is something between the donor and their maker.

Another TV show that makes for compulsive viewing is Secret Millionaire. You can watch a millionaire going undercover and then, if they like what they see, a charity wins as they get some dosh in a tearful, made for TV revelation. It cannot be disputed that giving so much money makes dreams come true. Such donations bring relief to the poor, of this there is no doubt—if I were running a charity I would probably be reduced to tears, so the charity workers should not be criticised—but how can this public act of such generous levels of giving be reconciled with the teaching to give in secret? How secret is it when you are proclaiming to the nation the level of your generosity? Perhaps it is unfair to judge the motives of these millionaires, but it is contrary to what I read in the Holy Bible. This may not matter to you if you have no faith, but couldn't they give without the TV cameras rolling? Perhaps they do, I don't know. Only God knows the heart of man.

In a round-about way I am trying to show that overall, in most societies, cash figures and values have become so important to many of us, whether this be in: business; socially; the media; or our churches. The Son of God, in his teaching, shows that valuing people by their wealth is a trap that we can all easily fall into. There is a far greater reward than five minutes of fame on a TV studio and holding up a large cheque for a few grand for the applause and appreciation of a few people.

So how much should we give, if anything at all? What should we tithe on a regular basis, if anything?

The answer to these questions will be very different to many people. If you have no faith, perhaps you are unsure as to what motivation there is to give. I know that when I had no faith, I had no motivation to give at all. I am certain that there are many, many people who are Atheist, Agnostic or whatever, who give, and give in abundance, and their motives are well intentioned. This desire to give is what I would define as the deep calling to the deep. And this gives us real hope! I believe that it is an inherent creator God who has given us a conscience, or what we can term as a God given depth of mercy, compassion and love. I believe that man, male and female were created in the image of God and one facet of God is one of mercy and compassion. Therefore, inherent within each one of us, as the ultimate of his creation, is this reflection of our creator, our Heavenly Father who is also merciful.

It goes without saying that many would disagree with this diagnosis, they are entitled to do so, but this is the starting point for me regarding our generosity. In creation at the very beginning of time—as we perceive time that is—man and woman are created as glorious creative beings and inherent within their spiritual DNA, is this Godly level of compassion and mercy. This DNA has then been passed on, from generation to generation, as part of the order of pro-creation.

Earlier in this book I have tried to show that God instructs the people of Israel to be compassionate to the stranger, the outcast, the down-trodden and the alien, and that this structure of social care was something that God desired for his chosen people. But God goes even further. Mercy and compassion are not just something of a vague ethereal and unobtainable concept, God makes this practical, to make our giving something that is solid, with foundation. There are numerous verses about giving of your best and not just in a random manner. We call this tithing. Let's try to narrow it down to a few basic principles by starting with the book of Leviticus and Chapter 27:

> [30]"A tithe of everything from the land, whether grain from the soil or fruit from the trees, belongs to the Lord, it is holy to the Lord…[32]every tenth that passes under the shepherd's rod—will be holy to the Lord. [33]He must not pick out the good from the bad or make any substitution. If he does make a substitution both the animal and its substitute become holy and cannot be redeemed."

When these few verses were recorded the Israelites were farmers. They grew crops, and they raised herds of sheep and goats, God demanded of them a tithe. The tithe was for the priests and for their sustenance; the poor; or just as an offering to God, because God is God. God asked them to give a tenth of what they grew and bred. This act of giving is something that is deemed to be an act of holiness. There is a consistent theme in the instructions for tithing, and general giving, in the Holy Bible, God asks us to do it willingly and cheerfully. For the livestock farmer there was a system of selection under the hand of God. A shepherd would hold out his rod or staff, some sheep would walk under it, those animals who walked under the staff were deemed as being God's and not the shepherd's. Even if a shepherd saw his show winning best of breed sauntering under the rod, they were forbidden from playing swapsies with God. Instead they were to trust in God within this selection process, and in God's ongoing provision.

Some Christians will cite the arbitrary rule of having to give ten percent of one's income as a regular tithe. But is it true that God requires this of us? Does he care whether we give ten percent, five percent, one hundred percent and whether this is of our gross or net income? Let's turn to Malachi and Chapter 3.

> [9]"…You are under a curse—the whole nation of you—because you are robbing me. [10]Bring the whole tithe into the storehouse, that there may be food in my house. Test me in this." says the LORD Almighty, "and see if I will not throw open the floodgates of heaven and pour out so much blessing that you will not have enough room for it…[12]Then all their nations will call you blessed, for yours will be a delightful land," says the LORD Almighty.

The people of God are short changing God so they are under a curse. These are very strong words of the prophet. The nation is neglecting the tithe, or if they are giving they are giving of their worst, or at least some of them are. It is a cycle. As the crops fail, the tithe becomes less, so the curse bites ever more, then the tithe becomes even less, the curse has an even greater effect, so the vicious circle continues. But, God says, if you give, then you will become more abundant, the curse will be lifted. The principle, for those of faith, is simple, give in faith, and trust that God will provide. I do not necessarily believe that God is cursing the land and the crops directly, it is more perhaps that he has the power to lift the drought as he is the omnipotent creator God.

This principle of total trust is alien to most of us, whether we have faith or not. In today's modern scientific world we find it hard to perceive that a land can be cursed, or that a nation could have such condemnation lifted by God, let alone that a country could lose some form of divine protection and blessing. And if we do believe that this is possible, we often think it is something that happened only in Biblical times. It is not something that would ever happen today; therefore such concepts hold no relevance.

I see and read of constants in the Biblical text, and this principle of us being thankful in giving of our best, willingly, to a faithful God is a catalyst to real redemption, even for a nation.

I do not believe that the poverty stricken in the world are under such a curse, it is the actions of the minority in this world that results in poverty. The poor are poor because we want to remain rich, as I have pointed out. So much poverty could be solved if only the excesses of the world's wealth were applied fairly to the problems that surround us. This abject poverty is a man-made curse of today, here and now. The failure of the few, to bring relief from poverty to the many, is an unhappy legacy. This speaks volumes about the collective nature of mankind. I wonder what our God in heaven thinks of our loss of holy giving, our collective hunger for wealth? What will befall the richer nations of the world when any form of God's protection is withheld, or becomes ever more distant.

Let's delve even further back into history—to a tale of many thousands of years earlier that I have already mentioned—that is about two brothers. Both of these brothers were farmers. One was an arable farmer, the other was a livestock farmer. They both offered to God the fruit of their labours, but one, he was called Cain, was jealous of his brother, who was called Abel. You may know this story, but let's look at what happened, and why, in the first book of the scriptures, Genesis and Chapter 4:

> ³In the course of time Cain bought some of the fruits of the soil as an offering to the LORD. ⁴But Abel brought fat portions from some of the firstborn of his flock. The LORD looked with favour on Abel and his offering, ⁵but on Cain and his offering he did not look with favour. So Cain was very angry, and his face was downcast.
>
> ⁶Then the LORD said to Cain, "Why are you angry? Why is your face downcast? ⁷If you do what is right, will you not be accepted? But if you do not do what is right, sin is crouching at your door; it desires to have you, but you must master it."

Firstly, consider the difference between the offerings. Abel offered the fat of his labours, the best of the firstborn of his herd. He picked out the fattest and the best firstborn of his flock out of gratitude to God. He did not hold back, he wanted to give to God the best that he had. His heart was in true fellowship with God. Now contrast this with Cain's offering. He brought along "some" crops. The text doesn't give them the same high status as Abel's, so we assume that they were not the ripest and most succulent. His face—both spiritually and physically—had made a journey from looking upward to God and he had become distracted by looking at the fat and plump offering of his brother. He was jealous of the willing attitude of his brother Abel. More than this though, he was angry with himself. His inward self loathing at his own failure required an outlet. He could see that his brother's heart was making an offering of thankfulness to God and he hated it. He just couldn't bring himself to make the same type of offering, that was choice number one down the Swanny. The second option had far more devastating consequences.

    Cain had lost sight of the point of the holy act of giving. God is God, he is the being who created matter out of nothing, he owns the earth and all that is in it, even you and I. God does not need any offering from us in order to exist. What offering can be made that can exalt God to a higher point than he already is? He is simply the great I AM. Offerings to God are seemingly pointless as they are insignificant in value when compared to the creator of all things. But still, he earnestly desires our offerings. He desires communion with us and our acknowledgement and gratitude of his rich vein of provision. This is not out of arrogance, but there is this inherent desire to be in deep relationship with us, the ultimate of his creation. God is a generous God, we are created in his image, therefore our generosity to one another and toward him is there, hidden deep within our very souls, though this has become corrupted and tainted over time by sin. The principle of giving is to give because giving is an act of holy worship and it mirrors the image of God. In the tale of Cain and Abel, look at what happens next, when sin possesses the heart of Cain.

> [8] Now Cain said to his brother Abel, "Let's go out to the field." And while they were in the field, Cain attacked his brother Abel and killed him.

Fratricide is committed. A man loses his life due to the jealous rage and anger that starts with self. The condition of the fallen and sinful human heart enters into this age old story and the consequences are dire.

Through the offering of Abel and through the seemingly small event where the widow offers everything, we witness the unison of two hearts. We witness hearts that make their respective offerings willingly, without reservation. These acts of holiness can be contrasted with the offering made by a man with utter resentment, reservation and anger. I see that the condition of the human heart in Abel was in union with the divine, virtually at the dawn of the age. The heart of a nameless widow was just as willing two thousand years ago. I witnessed the same willing heart in the little orphan boy when he gave up his last grain of Maize.

Through these stories I see a glimmer of hope. Occasionally a heart might appear in history that can teach us so very much that obliterates the deficiency of the fallen soul of the likes of Cain. We need to hold onto the offering of Abel, the widow and the orphan. We need to cling onto these examples with all of our might. Can you, will you emulate them by looking to your own heart? Are you willing to give beyond measure? Are you willing to give up all for the sake of a friend? And are you willing to do this in secret? When you do this there will be no acclamation, fanfares or applause, there will not even be a word of thanks from anyone. There will just be silence here on earth. But in heaven, that is a different story.

Giving is about giving freely, and cheerfully. Our gifts can be utilised to bring relief to the needy; the oppressed; the poor and the dispossessed.

We can ask how much should I give? Should it be from our net or gross income? Should we give regularly, as a tithe? But these are the wrong questions. When tithing is introduced, as a concept by God, there was no form of taxation as we know it. Therefore, in a sense, we are tithing from our income by paying a levy of tax, but ***this is not a willing tithe***. It is an imposition by government. I think that there is still room for a tithe that is made willingly, a deliberate act of generosity, something that we give freely. Such a gift says: I care; I want to help; I am not in this just for myself; I want to give something back so that others can benefit. Once we have established acts of willing generosity, the declaration that we should give an arbitrary set percentage over and above that of the taxes that the government collects from us is a poor argument. If we make the giving of an arbitrary figure a requirement of our faith, then we are living under an imposition of law and not one of grace.

Giving should be an act of grace and holiness. Western society has depleted their belief in God and as a consequence, we see that there is less of a need to give or tithe to the great I AM. Tithing is now often seen as being part of some kind of strict faith or religion, something that is old fashioned, almost cultic.

These concepts of fairness and generosity are far from the minds of most of us, let alone those of the Bankers.

I recall two instances of celebrity giving that does give us some reason to hope:

> The topic of giving was being discussed on a radio phone in, a lady had phoned in to say how they had tried to raise funds for some form of special wheelchair for a severely disabled child. The chair was going to cost thousands of pounds. They wrote to David and Victoria Beckham to ask for a donation. They received a letter back saying buy the chair and send them the bill.

Though this donation was made public by the recipients of the gift, the act of giving—by the Beckhams—was done in secret, quite silently. The second story revolves around Max Clifford the publicist to the stars. He also helps those who find themselves being thrust into the limelight as and when a story breaks.

He was also being criticised on a radio phone in show—quite heavily by a listener—for his allegedly money grabbing attitude. Impressively Max Clifford took this for a while and he responded quite lightly, trying to brush aside the criticism. The listener persisted in his condemnation and judgement.

Eventually Max Clifford firmly responded by pointing out that his charging structure to those of small means was little to nothing. He may even have said that it was nil in many cases. He also pointed out that he gives regularly to charitable causes out of his normal income. From memory this was a considerable percentage. He stated that he did not want to come out in public and say this, but as he was being criticised so vehemently in public he had no choice. The listener was silenced in their judgement.

In these examples the act of giving was silent and private. These celebs did not shout about it, or make a big public display of their wealth. Both, perhaps unknowingly, were adhering to the Biblical teaching of Christ, by giving in secret, and apparently willingly. For this they are to be applauded. Isn't this is a break in my argument though? Oh never mind. In essence, in the early Biblical times, giving to an early form of state benefits was voluntary. So, imagine for a moment that instead of paying taxes, you were asked to consider making a gift to a collective pot as a whole. These gifts could then be used to pay for education; health; a benefit system; a system of justice and law enforcement. Every need of society is then met by these gifts, instead of compulsion through a system of taxation. Is this too much to dream of?

[32]All the believers were one in heart and mind. No one claimed that any of his possessions was his own, but they shared everything they had...[34]There were no needy persons among them...

Would you like to dream the impossible with me? In this example above, from the book of Acts and Chapter 4, not one person of the new faith community of

Christians was in need. Yes it was just a few thousand people, but at that moment in history, a lifestyle choice was made. This community of believers were one in heart and they had established this fellowship under an act of holiness.

So where does all of this leave us? When Abel gave to God, there were no percentages involved. When the widow gave, she gave everything. When an orphan gave out of friendship, he gave his all. In all of these acts there is an intentional act. In contrast Cain was intent upon retribution and murder.

The ultimate sacrifice was that of Christ when he sacrificed himself upon the cross for he did not hold back. He didn't say, that's your lot, a nail through one hand and the whipping is my ten percent. That would have been an absurd level of sacrifice and an abomination that is greater than the scandal of the cross itself. The ultimate act of giving was Yeshua (Jesus) upon the cross, his descent into hell, his glorious resurrection and the cost of this was his all. We cannot even begin to match the enormity of this ultimate sacrifice in our giving, so if we are to emulate his own sacrifice, we should not try to out-give God, or give with any form of pride.

The rules of tithing a percentage was instigated because mankind was short changing God. Give me at least ten percent of your best God said, for that is better than nothing. But the church has, at least in the past, established a pattern of religiosity that has turned giving into a calculated chore.

I remember hearing talks—and attending Holy Bible studies—that wrestled with the issue of whether giving should be calculated upon one's gross or net income. How futile. I have arrived at the conclusion that this misses the point entirely, we should give because we want to. If we do not want to give, then don't. Radical I know, but at least it is an honest position to take up. The Psalmist touches upon this in Chapter 50 of the book of Psalms:

> [9]"I have no need of a bull from your stall
>   or of goats from your pens,
> [10]for every animal of the forest is mine,
>   and the cattle on a thousand hills.
> [11]I know every bird in the mountains,

> and the creatures of the field are mine.
> ¹²If I were hungry I would not tell you,
>> for the world is mine, and all that is in it.
> ¹³Do I eat the flesh of bulls
>> or drink the blood of goats?
> ¹⁴Sacrifice thank offerings to God,
>> fulfill your vows to the Most High,
> ¹⁵and call upon me in the day of trouble;
>> I will deliver you, and you will honour me."

For those of us who declare that we have a faith, our giving should be an act of worship, something incredibly holy, an acknowledgement of God, for God's sake. As I have said, God owns everything. This means that God owns the Bankers' bonuses; he owns the millions, billions and trillions that they invest upon our behalf and trade in, every single day. God owns the minerals that are mined and made into diamond rings; he owns the oil that fuels our cars; he owns the fields that provide our food etc… Once we have arrived at this position of acknowledgement and gratitude, then we will start to see and value our own wealth in a totally different light.

Why do I think that giving is intinsically linked to the credit crunch? Because once we perceive that wealth is transitory, once we see and understand that everything we own is not ours, we will begin to care less about valuations of pension, savings and investments. Once we are in this happy position, we will not care about what others earn, or how they use, or abuse, their wealth. We will also become more involved in the relief of poverty and we will value one another to a greater degree. We will then begin to see one another as equal. There is so much that will change once we become like Abel, the widow and the orphan.

> ⁷Each of you should give what you have decided in your heart to give, not reluctantly or under compulsion, for God loves a cheerful giver.

The above verse, from the book of Corinthians, Chapter 9, is not saying be jolly and full of jokes when you give money, it is saying be willing and contented that you are giving money. This means give it with no strings attached.

In contrast to the willing and giving hearts that we have examined in this chapter, we tend to maintain the concept that the city is there for the sole function of making money. There is nothing essentially wrong in investing in order to make a profit, it is apparent though that when God (or morality) is left out of the picture man has a problem of holding things in balance as greed often takes off unchecked.

We must generate and engender an attitude that says we care, we share in our wealth and good fortune, we are willing to be sacrificial as we share in your suffering, we wish to redeem the world from suffering. I say to the behemoth that is the financial market, time is up for your sole desire to make money; we call time upon your self interest; we challenge you and challenge you hard. Life is not just about profits for profits sake. A transformation is required for as we discover willing hearts and sacrificial giving, surely you will then work more for one another, and for your clients, than for self and self interest.

As a society we need to see a new generosity and a new level of fairness in the markets in order to move away from the false concept that wealth is the sole bringer of happiness.

So for each one of us, I pray that in our giving, we may become free and comfortable to give out of the generosity of our hearts, and that we may be free to give whatever we want, whenever we want, and that we may discover our own secret and quiet act of holy worship.

CHAPTER NINE

GREEDY BLEEPING BLEEPERS

So how big are all of these bonuses that the Bankers are receiving? Firstly it is quite hard to pin down as to exactly who is receiving what, but it is probably safe to assume that the average bank clerk is not in receipt of huge bonuses that are paid out each year. The problem with much of the headlines of the past year or so is that some are misleading. For example when you see a headline—as I did recently—that around 100 so called Bankers are going to receive a bonus of £1 million each, this may appear to be obscene, but there is more behind the headlines. This same bank employs around 90,000 people in the U.K. alone, yet only 100 of the staff are in line for the bonus! Can this be justified?

Perhaps this is not so much about whether a taxpayer owns a bank or not, and whether bonuses are unfair, it is more about equality—or rather the lack of it. How can an employer pay out such a large level of bonuses to less than 1% of its workforce!

But this is nothing new, large bonuses have always been on offer. In 2006, 11 senior executives at the firm Goldman Sachs were given a tad over a combined total of $150 million. However, this is not just a cash bonus, as it consisted of some shares and stock. This is something that the media does not report. The daily media tends to say that Bankers have received an outrageous amount of many millions, often these bonuses are not paid out in cash. (These options and shares may now be worthless, and many of us might gain some satisfaction from this.) These particular bonuses to these executives were awarded on the back of a rise on net profits of 70%. It could be argued that the bonuses are well deserved on the back of these large profits. At the time of awarding these executive bonuses, the company set aside $16.5 billion for all staff bonuses!

But the bonus culture does not stop there. In 2009 it was estimated that Goldman Sachs, Morgan Stanley and JPMorgan were to hand out, in bonuses, a combined total of $29.7 billion. This was an increase of 60% on the previous year and it would be a record award. This was to be split between a total of around 119,000 employees equating to around $250,400 each employee. This bonus is five times greater than the average level of household income—in the U.S. in 2008—of $50,303. Paul Hodgson, a senior research associate on compensation (bonuses) at the Portland Maine based Corporate Library said in an email:

> Wall Street is beginning to resemble Clark Gable as Rhett Butler in the film: Gone With the Wind, 'Quite Frankly, my dear, I don't give a damn.' It doesn't seem as if even political threat, disastrous PR, envy, rising unemployment rates and home repossessions is enough to get any of these people to refuse the bonuses they have 'earned'.[xviii]

Has anything changed since 2009? Not really no. According to a survey, that was carried out recently, by a well known financial careers company, showed that:

> The omens for 2010 compensation aren't good, but this didn't appear to trouble any of the 5,671 global and 537 U.K. based financial services employees who responded to our bonus survey this year…
>
> …57% of U.K. financial services professionals expect to receive a larger bonus for 2010 than 2009. 17% of people expect their bonus to increase by more than 50%… In the US only 50% of respondents were expecting their bonus to increase. In Singapore and Hong Kong 69% and 71% respectively are expecting an increase…[xix]

Just a year earlier (2009) Mark Borges, a compensation consultant for Compensia Inc, in California said that Wall Street is behaving like:

> We made it through the storm, and now it's back to doing things we know how to do in our comfortable environment. It really runs counter to the things you're hearing out of the administration, about how things have to change.

[xviii] Please see more on this story at: http://www.bloomberg.com/apps/news?pid=newsarchive&sid=aR0E6lSBRfs8
[xix] Please see more on this story at: http://news.efinancialcareers.co.uk/News_ITEM/newsItemId-28789

In October 2010 it was reported that:

> U.S. Bankers are set for record compensation for a second consecutive year…
>
> With third-quarter figures from JPMorgan expected to begin a bumper profit reporting season today, a study of more than three dozen banks, hedge funds, money-management and securities firms, estimates they will pay $144 billion in salary and benefits this year, a 4% increase on 2009.
>
> The research, by the Wall Street Journal, found pay was rising faster than revenue, which gained 3% to £433 billion…[xx]

In amongst these headlines it is staggering that when we examine the news behind the headlines, pay on Wall Street is set to break previous remuneration records! This is a different world to that of most of us. These banking institutions have been bailed out by the governments of the world, yet they continue to pay massive bonuses, which are expected by so many. In the same article—in The Guardian—Charles Elson Director of the Weinberg centre for Corporate Governance is reported to have said, to the Wall Street Journal:

> Until the focus of these institutions change from revenue generation to long-term shareholder value, we will see these outrageous pay packages and [bonus] levels [continue]…

This is exactly what my friend Derek points out (please see the chapter entitled: the Fight Back). Investment managers need to take a longer term view and build real capital value into investments rather than looking for high risk short term gains. I also believe that one of the intrinsic problems within the markets, regulation and economic policy of countless governments, throughout the world is that the whole system operates a bit like an old fashioned club. Promotion is often from within, or across the differing spheres of responsibility. For example, one Henry Paulson was given $38.3 million in bonuses in 2005. Shortly afterward he accepted the post of

---

[xx] Please see more on this story at: http://www.guardian.co.uk/business/2010/oct/12/us-bankers-record-pay-bonuses

U.S. Treasury Secretary. This appointment was made by George Bush. There have been other similar "inside" appointments both in the U.S. and the U.K. It can be argued that those who have worked within the financial sector know about the peculiarities and machinations of the sector and that such people are best placed to regulate and oversee it. In the current climate I do not think that this is necessarily the case. I would suggest that some distance and impartiality needs to be established between the Bankers, the regulator and those in government.

Apart from anything else, how do these employers expect to engender loyalty in firms that embrace such a structure of large bonuses for the few. With so much wealth on display it should not come as too much of a surprise that Jot—the PA to wealthy Bankers—was convicted of robbing her bosses.

Perhaps these excesses are to blame for cultivating an arrogance within the financial cities of the world. It is hard, for most of us to understand how, when working under such a rewarding bonus structure, one very high profile boss of the largest banking institution in the world could say that:

I'm doing God's work.

I look at servants of God in the Holy Bible, few are wealthy. The ancient King that we call Solomon was pretty wealthy—perhaps a few others like him—but in general the likes of the prophets of old and people such as John the Baptiser were all pretty poor. Many Christian's believe that they are doing a work to which God has called them to, but when this particular boss claims to be doing the will of God, here on earth, I am compelled to examine this claim in more detail.

The man who said that he was performing the will of God is one Lloyd Blankfein. Firstly we must bear in mind that his reported earnings for the year 2007/08 were in excess of $72 million! This level of earnings was apparently a record for Wall Street. In 2009/10 his total remuneration is vastly reduced. It is reported to have been just $862,657. I wonder how you feel at his drop in salary of over 98%? Imagine if your own income dropped by this amount, how would you cope? But here is the rub, he still has over $800,000 to play with! If your income dropped by such a percentage, how much would you have left? To be fair to him, Blankfein later claimed that he was joking when he made the declaration that invoked the Almighty. But then again, others took this one step further and they took it seriously.

According to a transcript of a meeting of the St Paul's Institute at St Paul's Cathedral on Tuesday 20th October 2009, the International Adviser to Goldman Sachs, Brian Griffiths, said:

> I think that the injunction of Jesus to love others as ourselves is a recognition of self-interest...
>
> I'm a person of hope, and I think that we have to tolerate the inequality as a way to achieving greater prosperity and opportunity for all.[xxi]

These thoughts of the city do not stop there. John Varley, The Chief Executive Officer of Barclays Plc—Britain's second-biggest bank—made the news by standing at the wooden lectern in St. Martin-in-the-Fields in Trafalgar Square by declaring that within banking:

> There is no conflict between doing business in an ethical and responsible way and making money. We make our biggest contribution to society by being good at what we do...profit is not satanic.[xxii]

Some of what these good folk say is correct. There is nothing wrong in making money, ethically, profit is not the work of the devil, but it is this claim of the moral high ground that gets to many of us, especially when the Bankers are, in part, responsible for the mess that we are in. You cannot argue morality and ethics when we have seen the collapse of the likes of Lehmann Brothers and Bear Sterns due to Bankers utter stupidity, negligence and incompetence. It is a bit like asking King Herod the Great to be a god-parent to your children. You would only do it under duress and with trepidation knowing that things might get to be a bit tricky with

---

[xxi] Please download the entire transcript at: http://www.stpauls.co.uk/documents/st%20paul's%20institute/regulation%20freedom%20and%20human%20welfare%20transcript.pdf
[xxii] Please read more on this story at: http://www.dailymail.co.uk/news/article-1225285/Profit-satanic-says-Barclays-boss.html

Uncle Herod being in charge of your kids spiritual well-being!

Let's take a closer look at these morals. Look in the scriptures with me (there is more of this later as well):

> ⁷If anyone is poor among your fellow Israelites in any of the towns of the land the LORD your God is giving you, do not be hardhearted or tightfisted toward them. ⁸Rather, be open handed and freely lend them whatever they need.[xxiii]

> ⁷…share your food with the hungry
> …provide the poor wanderer with shelter—
> when you see the naked…clothe them…[xxiv]

> ³³Sell your possessions and give to the poor. Provide purses for yourselves that will not wear out, a treasure in heaven that will never fail, where no thief comes near and no moth destroys.[xxv]

> ⁴²Give to the one who asks you, and do not turn away from the one who wants to borrow from you.[xxvi]

Taking these verses in turn (and risking taking them out of context), did the banks lend freely, that is, with no interest? Are the banks now tightfisted in their lending policies? Next. When was the last time a wealthy Banker declined their bonus in order to give it to the hungry, poor and dispossessed? Next. When did a Banker last sell their possessions to gain a treasure outside of this physical reality? And finally; did the banks lend honestly, openly, sensibly and fairly?

How one can claim that the structure of the investment banks and city institutions and the current bonus structure is in line with any of this teaching is puzzling. These Bankers must be reading a different version of the holy text to me. Now think for a

---

[xxiii] Please see the book of Deuteronomy, Chapter 15.
[xxiv] Please see the book of Isaiah, Chapter 58.
[xxv] Please see the book of Luke, Chapter 12.
[xxvi] Please see the book of Matthew, Chapter 5.

moment about the remuneration of Lloyd Blankfein and his $72 million earned in one solitary year. Is this really in line with Biblical teaching? What if we contrast his pay package with that of another man who claimed to be carrying out the will of God, the one called Yeshua (Jesus)? I hope that you get the point. This denial by high level executives that they are not doing, or have not done, anything wrong—and their going one step further by claiming a strange morality—is an odd claim to make. There is also an implication that nothing needs to be addressed within the system at large, including the bonus structures. This is a strange view that is divorced from my own understanding of scripture.

During a recent conversation with another friend in the city, we landed upon this very issue of bonuses. He said this to me:

> I would hope, that if I were living on a desert island, with my wife and children, that I would be able to be happy, with the bare essentials of food, shelter and water.

I wonder. Would he, or I, really be happy, with no email, internet, TV etc? Would you be happy? Would the banking executives be happy? To argue that the system needs to be maintained with inequality in order to gain prosperity (bear in mind that this is said by people who have enormous amounts of wealth, would they spout the same ridiculous philosophy if they were at the other end of the scale?). They also imply that this prosperity is available to all, and that this state of inequality is compatible with God's word. This is all contrary to what I read of within the pages of an arbitrator that speaks volumes about of the redemption of the poor. The logic of this argument of the banking executives is that we have a perverse God who created a high order of intelligence and then decided that some are to remain homeless and poor, whilst others can be wealthy, but that is your lot. If the poor become wealthier, then we need more poor people to be put in their place and this will maintain a healthy balance of inequality. This type of God would not be worthy of any praise or acknowledgement for they would be no better than you or I.

It is this perception of many in the city—whether they be Bankers, investors, financiers, economists and even the politicians, who justify their role by maintaining that extreme wealth is good because it will drip feed down through the lower echelons of society—that is a perverse concept. But, it is a concept that is maintained and argued for time and time again. This mind-set has corrupted the world's markets by becoming embedded in the psyche of the workers in the city, the regulators and the legislators. Just how this perception can be broken, I do not really know, but surely it must be broken, for the good of all, and we must seek a higher way.

Let's look at a few other stories as to how these institutions have behaved. We will stick with the largest banking institution in the world, Goldman Sachs. This particular bank has become besieged with accusations of fraud and immorality. The men at the very top are being hunted down, even by the U.S. Senate. They have faced hour upon hour of questioning by the lawmakers across the pond, as they face the charge of putting their own interests before the interest of their clients. (We are back to the adage of my own mentor: remember whose money it is!) A basic policy of this investment bank appears to have been the wrapping up of the rather dubious lending policies of the banks at large—and their subsequent loans—into a neat bundle that in turn became a rather dodgy investment product. In some of these products, as many as 90% of the associated loans and mortgages that were bundled into these complex investments, had been written on a so-called:

…stated income basis.

This means that homeowners were not required to offer any proof of their salaries on their mortgage applications. Of course, this type of practice was not the exclusive domain of banks in the U.S., or of financial institutions of the size of Goldman Sachs.

In a recent senate hearing an allegation was levied that the executives at Goldman Sachs created and sold extremely complex mortgage backed investment securities that were branded—by their own employees—as being:

…shitty…and…crap pools…

At this senate hearing one Dan Sparks, who was previously the head of the bank's mortgage unit, conceded:

We made a number of poor business decisions, especially in hindsight.

Poor business decisions, that must be the understatement of the millennium. They were more than just poor risk based decisions, even their own traders knew that some of their products were "shit" as they so aptly said in correspondence to one another.

This senate hearing also saw the public appearance and the questioning of a rather interesting character, one Fabrice Tourre. As an employee, of Goldman Sachs based in London, he masterminded an investment deal that the bank proudly called: Abacus. The Securities and Exchange Commission has stated that this particular deal was fraudulent. Fabrice Tourre has rejected this serious charge. These charges will no doubt be fought over when they are fully investigated and whether this product was fraudulent, under the law, is yet to be proven.

But, within some e.mails to his girlfriend—that had been made public prior to the senate hearing—Fabrice Toure had appeared to ridicule his own work as he referred to it as:

…Intellectual masturbation…

And some products he likened to the production of:

…Frankenstein.[xxvii]

Goldman Sachs appears to have given many names to their products. Another investment package was called: Anderson. This product was downgraded from a top rating of triple A, to the abysmal rating of junk, within just a few short months! Despite this useless rating being applied, Goldman Sachs invited their clients to invest. There was also the $1 billion package with the macho name of: Timberwolf. This was branded, in an internal email by Thomas Montag—the then head of sales and trading for the Americas, at Goldman Sachs—as being a:

[xxvii] Please read more on this story at:
http://www.guardian.co.uk/business/2010/apr/27/goldman-sachs-senate-committee-hearing

…shitty deal.

When questioned about these products and the email correspondence of their executives, the bank's financial officer, David Viniar, replied:

> I think that's very unfortunate to have on email.

I find this statement staggering and unsurprisingly this apparently nonchalant answer elicited audible gasps from those at the hearing in the U.S. Senate. I am also speechless at this attitude. (For me to be at a loss for words is something that occurs very rarely!) The point is this, there is no apparent repentance, regret or sorrow for what they did, with hard working investors money.

Later, the chief executive at Goldman Sachs—Lloyd Blankfein—continued to insist that the views of his bank about the doomed state of some of the complex financial products that they offered to investors was of little relevance to those who bought into these products. He is reported to have said that:

> The thing customers are buying is exposure. The thing they're buying gives them the risk they want. They're not coming to us because of what our views are.

Allegedly, this particular bank designed products that were doomed and useless. When it went pear shaped, they hid behind the fact that clients wanted risk and that Investment Bankers were just a tool in giving clients what they wanted. Rightly or wrongly, he has tried to abdicate responsibility.

In amongst all of this, it is true that the bonuses being taken by staff were high. The hearing questioned why this was the case when matters were going awry. It was down to the enigmatic Farbice Tourre to defend the venerable and old institution, Goldman Sachs:

> To the average person, the utility of these products may not be obvious. But they permit sophisticated institutions to customise the exposures they wish to take in order to better manage the credit and market risks of their investment holdings.

He is implying that the average person is unable to understand the products, so leave it to us, as we are sophisticated and educated enough to understand what is going on even when you cannot. He has firmly taken up the mantra of exposure = importance (see the following chapter for more on this). Is this why bonuses have to be so high?

Some of what has essentially gone wrong is the relationship of trust within complex products that few have understood. To invest we do not need to understand everything, but we do need to be able to trust those who work on our behalf. If I have a builder erect an extension on my house upwards, or lengthways, I do not understand anything about foundations, electric cabling, gas and water pipes. But I do need to be able to trust that the builder will work honestly, and to the best of their ability. It is this foundation of trust that has been shot to pieces by some of the financial institutions.

To liken an investment product that you are promoting to that of "masturbation", apart from being very crude, it is staggering and well beyond my comprehension that someone could be so blasé about their work. To give him some credit Fabrice Tourre has issued statements of regret for these words, but the question remains; why did he apparently write such derogatory statements in the first place?

Goldman Sachs' employees, right to the very top, continue to deny that they have done anything illegal or wrong.

This story has not reached a conclusion yet, for Goldman Sachs has survived the crisis despite being levied fines by the regulators of astronomical proportions, both in the U.S. and here in the U.K. In July 2010, Goldman Sachs agreed to pay a fine of a staggering $550 million (around £356 million) in order to settle outstanding civil fraud charges of misleading investors. This includes a fine against the investment bank for the conduct of the staff involved in the investment product that Goldman Sachs had called Abacus. The financial watchdog—in the U.S.—the: Securities and Exchange Commission said that this was:

...the biggest fine for a bank in its history.

Whether they should be proud of levying such a fine is open to question. Some are now asking just what were the regulators doing while all of this activity was going on? Secondly it is an agreed fine, there seems to be little real imposition in this fiasco by the regulator. Despite the amount of the fine appearing to be so huge, in reality it is peanuts to the bank. When examining some of the reported figures of the balance sheet of Goldman Sachs for 2009 they are reported as follows:

Staff Pay	$16.2 billion
Profits	$12.2 billion
US Government support	$10.0 billion
Fine	$550 million

Despite having this record fine levied against them, the shares in Goldman Sachs rose by 4.5% soon after the news of this fine broke! This rise in share price of the investment bank is a reflection of the opinion that many in the financial sectors felt that the firm had got off lightly. One city bod is reported to have said:

They pay $550 million and they get an $800 million pop in their stock price… they got off easy…[xxviii]

Furthermore, Goldman Sachs made a profit of $3.5 billion in the first three months of 2010! But who gets the money from the fine? The Royal Bank of Scotland (RBS), in the U.K.—84% of which is owned by the U.K. government—will receive $100 million compensation as RBS lost about $840 million on investments that they placed with Goldman Sachs. This return is a paltry amount compared to their losses. A German bank, IKB Deutsche Industriebank, will receive around $150 million. This means that they will recoup all of the losses they incurred on the flawed Abacus investment. The rest of the fine? The U.S. Treasury gets the lions share of around $300 million!

There are a lot of figures to take in here, but I hope that you get the gist of what has gone on here. A respected investment bank dreams up a "shitty" product (their

---

[xxviii] Please read more on this story at: http://www.reuters.com/article/idUSTRE66E60G20100715

words not mine), they get large institutions to invest; when it is proved to be a useless investment they are called up before a U.S. Senate hearing they are then fined an amount that is miniscule when comparing it to their profits; they continue to pay their staff (at least some of them) very well and despite everything—including the bad publicity—they produce record profits during the year 2009.

Would you invest, today, here and now, into Goldman Sachs, if you were given the opportunity to do so? Amazingly people are still trusting Goldman Sachs. And again when looking at some figures, one can see why. The much derided Abacus investment lost a little more than $1 billion (around £650 million) when the U.S. housing market collapsed. Overall, when viewing the profits of this company, this loss is nothing to the Bank. It is shameful to say it, and this is what makes this fiasco significant, it is inevitable that they will survive, but, and here's the rub, for the sake of all of us they must do so. If this global bank were to go under such a calamity would affect both you and me quite drastically. We would experience a desolate impact upon our pensions, savings and investments. It is not easy just to say that these banks, and their employees, should be left to sink or swim. Our economies and the very basics of our lifestyles, are so intertwined and dependent upon such institutions, as Goldman Sachs. Whether they should be so linked is another matter. I would argue that having such a large institution is unhealthy, as we cannot afford to allow these monoliths to fail.

This is of concern but it goes so very much deeper than even this. The poor sods—many of whom were, and remain, uneducated and illiterate—were wrapped up in grand schemes like the Abacus product and they have literally lost everything. They had taken out mortgage loans, with no proof of income, believing that they were living out the great American dream. Yes we are all responsible for our own actions, but when a sharp suited sales person calls to your run down home, when they use words that you barely understand to convince you to sign up; and when these salesmen and women assure you that all is well in believing in the dream of home ownership, many will inevitably fall for the patter. It has become apparent that people did trust and sign up, in their thousands. Now these same people are poverty stricken and homeless.

It is all very well for the U.S. government, and other regulators throughout the world, levying fines and offering bailouts to enable the general economy of the world to survive, this is essential for our own continuing economic stability, but what of the repossessed? What do they get out of this? The answer is nothing at all.

When examining the financial systems of the world, one still questions what went wrong? I believe it was nothing more than greed. Greed for bonuses, greed to amass wealth of millions each year, in these salaries and bonuses. This is also apparent when a so called Banker is so arrogant as to declare that when they are in receipt of such bonuses, it is God's work that they are undertaking (even though this may have been meant as a joke it is not that funny to the repossessed and homeless!). But this endemic nature of greed has been the case for years. I can point to another infamous story of the 1980s:

> It was the buzzing, exciting, boom years of the 80s. Aspiring city traders were young, the bonus culture was alive and well. Avarice and acquiring wealth was seen as being good.
>
> A working class lad from Watford, the son of a humble plasterer, was delighted when he managed to land a job in the financial capital of the world, London, in 1982.
>
> His first job was that of a minion. He soon made a name for himself. He worked hard for long hours. He became a whizz-kid in the far Eastern currency markets.
>
> He became a star trader for his employer. He bought in substantial profits from the Singapore International Monetary Exchange.
>
> By 1993, just one year after his arrival in Asia, he allegedly made about 10% of his employers total profit for that year! He was an astounding achiever.
>
> Both he and his wife enjoyed a life of luxury that most of us can only dream of.
>
> In 1994, his luck began to change. The markets turned against him. The downturn that the world was experiencing was accelerated by the economic

impact of an earthquake in Kobe, Japan.

By the autumn of the same year, his losses could no longer be hidden. But he was determined to see it through. He had seen through other problems, surely he could do the same again. He requested extra funds to enable him to continue his trading activities. His request was granted, after all he was the star of the team. Frenetically he attempted to extricate himself from the financial mess of his own making by launching himself into more and more deals.

Finally his bosses, who had become concerned by his requests for more money, carried out a spot audit in February of the following year. They soon discovered, to their horror, that the losses of this one trader amounted to such a level that they amounted to almost more than the entire assets of the bank!

He had hidden the losses that he had incurred in an obscure account called: Error Account 88888.

He and his wife went on the run, finally giving himself up, in Germany. He was extradited to Singapore and he pleaded guilty to fraud. He was sentenced to six and a half years in prison.

The bank that boasted that it had HM Queen Elizabeth II on its books, the oldest merchant bank in the U.K., could not survive such losses. Finally, it crashed.

Dozens of executives who were implicated in the failure to control this rogue trader resigned or were subsequently sacked.

This rogue trader was released from prison in 1999. Since his release he has overcome a bout of cancer, remarried. He now lives in Ireland, he is the author of several books and he has carved out a new career as a speaker.[xxix]

I am sure that you now recall the name of the bank, and the rogue trader who hit the headlines. It was Nick Leeson and his employer was Barings Bank. This was such a high profile case at the time and it remains an intriguing case. It must be

---

[xxix] Please read more on this story at: http://www.nickleeson.com/biography/index.html

acknowledged that Nick Leeson was a completely different type of trader to that of Fabrice Tourre at Goldman Sachs, nevertheless, surely the driving factor was the same, for both men?

But there is another significant difference between Fabrice Tourre—the other executives of Goldman Sachs—and Nick Leeson. It is that those within Goldman Sachs, who are under the spotlight at this time, are still in denial of any wrongdoing. Perhaps they have been advised to admit nothing by their sharp suited and highly paid lawyers, as they do not want to go to prison! In contrast, Nick Leeson has admitted wrongdoing and he once said this:

> We were all driven to make profits, profits, and more profits…I was the rising star.

As I have said, we are responsible for our own actions, but in the trading desks (whether it be in the 1980s or in more recent times), there has been this growth in this sense of urgency to make profits today, here and now, for short term growth is good.

Having worked in the financial services sector for a number of years (though I am nowhere near the status of any sort of trader) and having met several analysts, Bankers and investment gurus, I believe that this short termism is wrong. This is a misplaced and dangerous concept. But this whole environment creates opportunities for huge bonuses in the short term. If only the financial sector had adopted a culture of sacrifice, valuing one another and who we are, perhaps this culture of high bonuses and the inherent belief that wealth is good for all and so we must tolerate inequality, would never have arisen. It is this inherent expectation and hunger for profits that drive the monster that we call the financial markets. Little thought is given over to what the consequences might be for taking high risks. For the sake of profit we all want to take a collective risk, but we are rarely prepared to suffer the potential losses!

Whilst we, Bankers and investors alike, retain this hunger for wealth the cycle is unlikely to change. There will inevitably be another Nick Leeson, Fabrice Tourre and more "shit" products at some point. Human nature will not change until the mantle of sacrificial morality is taken up. To me there is a need to work under the authority of a divine being, and his word, the ultimate arbitrator, the Holy Bible.

This desire to drive matters forward with the sole aim of making money, to accumulate wealth, is nothing new. I have mentioned the South Sea Bubble scam, well here is the tale of perhaps the most infamous scam in history. This con really goes to the heart of fallen mankind, abject greed:

> One Charles Ponzi was born on March 3rd in 1882. An Italian immigrant who arrived—on November 15th in the year 1903—aboard the S.S. Vancouver in Boston, in the land of opportunity and dreams, the good ole' U.S. of A. He was to become one of the greatest (if that's the right word) con-men in American—if not world—history.
>
> By his own account, Ponzi landed with two dollars and fifty cents in his pocket, having gambled away the rest of his savings during the voyage. In an interview in the New York Times he said:
>
>> I landed in this country with $2.50 in cash and $1 million in hopes, and those hopes never left me.

He soon became fluent in English. He spent the next few years doing odd jobs along the East Coast of America, finally landing a job as a dishwasher in a restaurant where he slept on the floor at night. He worked his way up to the position of waiter. He was fired when he was caught short changing the customers and stealing.

In 1907, Ponzi moved to Canada, where became an assistant teller in a newly opened bank. This bank paid a savings rate that was double the normal rate of interest on accounts. (Would you have plunged in there with your own savings—or would you have said no way, it's too good to be true?) Unsurprisingly the bank took in money easily from investors. Ponzi soon discovered that the bank was in serious financial trouble because of bad loans (does this sound familiar?). The bank's owner was funding interest payments to investors, not through profits, but by using money deposited in newly opened accounts. The bank would take money from customer B to pay interest at the high rate to customer A; the money from customer C was used to pay customer B, and so on. But when you get to the metaphorical customer Z there are no other customers. Inevitably the bank failed. The owner of the bank fled to Mexico with a large wodge of the investors money.

Ponzi stuck around. To his credit he tried to help the previous bank owners abandoned family. Perhaps at the same time the germ of an idea had come to the mind of Ponzi. He was flat stone broke. Eventually he forged the signature of a company director—on a cheque that belonged to a bank client, in a cheque book that he had found lying around in the bank—to the tune of $423.58. When confronted by police Ponzi held out his hands, wrists upward. He immediately admitted his guilt.

For this crime—which was pretty minor when compared to what was to come—he spent three years in a prison in Canada. Like a loyal Italian son, he kept in touch with his Momma. He wrote telling her that he had found a job as a special assistant to a prison warden. He failed to mention that he was a prisoner!

Ponzi was released from prison in 1911. He decided to go southwards and back to the land of opportunity. Had his spell in prison reformed him? Far from it. He soon became embroiled in a scheme that smuggled Italian illegal immigrants into America. He was caught and was back in jail, this time in Atlanta for two years.

During this spell of incarceration he had time to reflect. He became a translator for the prison warden, who was intercepting letters from the Italian mobster Lupo the Wolf. Ponzi eventually ended up befriending Lupo. No doubt this was another influence upon his future.

Ponzi also came to know another prisoner, Charles Morse, formerly a Wall Street businessman and speculator. In 1910 Morse was sent to prison for various white collar crimes, but in 1912 he became very ill. A panel of Army doctors declared that he was suffering from a condition that required specialist treatment and prison was no place for a man in his condition. He was granted a pardon and he departed the penitentiary for urgent medical treatment. However, it soon became apparent that Morse had fooled doctors during his medical examination by poisoning himself by eating soap shavings. The toxins left his body almost as quickly as the doctors had left his bedside.

So far, in the few years that Ponzi had lived in America, he had encountered a corrupt Banker; a mobster; and a convicted Wall Street speculator. One can only imagine the influence that such relationships would have had upon him.

Eventually, post prison, an idea occurred to him. This was not a new idea, but it was to eventually net so much money that it was the first scam of its kind to become known throughout the United States, and beyond. He may have been inspired by a book-keeper from Brooklyn, William Miller who, in 1899, had used a similar pyramid scheme to fleece $1 million off gullible investors. In the novel Little Dorrit (published in 1857), Charles Dickens also described a similar type of scam.

The scheme that Ponzi engaged in was simple. Since 1906 many countries across the world agreed that an International Reply Coupon (IRC) bought in one country, could be redeemed in another country, even though there may be a real terms price difference between the two countries due to exchange rates and cost of living variations. Therefore there was a profit that could be made by taking advantage of the differing postal rates in different countries, so Ponzi decided to buy an IRC cheaply in one country, exchange them for stamps for a larger value in another country, thereby generating profits. In practice, however, in order to make any substantial profits, Ponzi would have had to purchase a vast quantity of IRCs. Even with such a large volume of purchases the profit margins would have been minute, partly due to the overheads involved. Despite the flaws in the scheme, Ponzi managed to convince his friends to invest. He promised investors a large profit within 45 days, or a considerable profit within 90 days. Quite clearly this was impossible to achieve, but there is one born every minute the old adage goes. He explained to his investors that the great returns available from IRCs was easy money! (If it was so easy to do, why didn't they do it themselves instead of using a go between?)

The initial investors were paid, as promised. Word spread like wildfire. Ponzi hired agents and he paid them very generous commissions.

Within a short period of time he had made millions. Investors were doing anything to get a piece of the action. They mortgaged their homes and invested their life savings. Due to greed, most investors did not take their profits, but they simply reinvested.

On the surface all seemed rosy. Ponzi, and his sales team were literally swimming in wealth, for he lived in sheer luxury. He bought a mansion in Lexington that had air-con and a heated swimming pool, an absolute extravagance at the time. He maintained accounts in several banks across New England. He also paid for his mother's passage, from Italy, in a first-class stateroom on an ocean liner. She died soon afterward—but at least she died happy and proud of her son!

But in reality, the whole operation was running at a large loss. As long as the money kept flowing in, existing investors could be paid. Just like the banking boss Ponzi had previously worked for. He had calculated that if you took investment monies from Client A, he could pay the promised returns by using money from client B; the money from client C would be used to pay client B and so on. In reality new investors money was the only source that Ponzi had to pay off existing investors. Legitimate profits, well they were impossible. (Does this remind you of Goldman Sachs and their wrapping up investors money and loans, in complex products and selling them onto others?)

Some started to question and wonder how this Italian emigré could have risen from penury to the status of being a multi-millionaire in such a short period of time? A financial journalist in Boston suggested there was no way on earth that this man, and his scheme, could legally deliver such high returns in such a short space of time. Ponzi promptly sued the journalist for libel and he must have been delighted when he won $500,000 in damages. The libel law at the time placed the burden of proof upon the reporter and his paper. Both had no real proof, just a hunch that the scheme was flawed. By winning this lawsuit Ponzi managed to stave off the inevitable, for a while.

Despite this apparent good fortune, cracks had started to appear in his enterprise. A Boston furniture dealer had supplied Ponzi furniture which Ponzi could not afford to pay for. The dealer attempted to sue Ponzi. He failed in his attempt. But more questions were asked. A run on one of Ponzi's investments began. Some investors decided to pull out. Ponzi paid them in full and the run stopped as quickly as it had started. On July 24th in 1920, the Boston Post printed a favourable article on Ponzi and his scheme. Once again investors clamoured for yet more of the action.

It is reported that Ponzi was making around $250,000 each and every day! Due to such good publicity Ponzi arrived at his office to find literally thousands of Bostonians eager to give him their money. Ponzi could not say no, for the only way he could maintain the payment of such high returns was through new investors money.

Despite all of this apparently high level of success, some journalists remained suspicious. Investigators were assigned to check Ponzi out. He was also under investigation by the Commonwealth of Massachusetts. He managed to divert the officials from checking his books by offering to stop taking money during the investigation. Had they known that no proper records were in existence the entire scam would have come to crashing to a sharp halt there and then, but this co-operative offer calmed the suspicions of the state officials.

The reporters finally started to unravel the truth. One particular reporter had done their sums. They had worked out that to cover the investments made with one of Ponzi's outfits, the Old Colony Foreign Exchange Company, then a massive 160 million postal reply coupons would have had to be in circulation! However, only around 27,000 were available.

An angry crowd gathered outside his offices, but Ponzi sweet talked the crowd. He ordered coffee and doughnuts all round, he informed investors that there was nothing wrong. He paid out $2 million in three days. Many of the investors changed their minds. Unwisely they left their money invested.

However, this activity did not escape the notice of the attorney for the district of Massachusetts. He commissioned an audit of the company's books. This was a tricky exercise as the book-keeping of Ponzi was a system of index cards with investors names on them. That was it.

Eventually the money ran out. Despite Ponzi's best efforts to stave off the final demise of his empire. He even hired a publicity agent who later shopped him and later called Ponzi a financial idiot who could not add up. Ponzi was arrested and he pleaded guilty to mail fraud.

His fraudulent activity bought down five banks!

Due to the exploits of Ponzi, the type of pyramid scheme that he engaged in became universally known as a Ponzi scheme.

Ponzi was never reformed, he went on to involve himself in other various fraudulent dealings. Before he died he granted a final interview to a reporter. An apparently unrepentant Ponzi said:

> Even if they never got anything for it, it was cheap at that price. Without malice aforethought I had given them the best show that was ever staged in their territory since the landing of the Pilgrims! It was easily worth fifteen million bucks to watch me put the thing over.

You would think that people would have learned their lesson wouldn't you. I shall not bother to enter into the full details of the recent story of Bernard Madoff, the guy who was running a pyramid, or Ponzi, scheme and the estimated $50 billion (or more) that he scammed from respected institutions. Suffice it to say that at one point in his career Bernard Madoff sat on the Board of Directors of the Securities Industry Association, which merged with the Bond Market Association in 2006 to form the Securities Industry and Financial Markets Association (SIFMA) who are the trade body that represents securities firms; banks; asset management companies etc… Madoff was a highly respected individual in the financial world, as was his family, yet he was essentially running a huge Ponzi scheme! He had recognition, status and wealth. Morality cannot have been on his horizon. People believed that he was one of the good guys! How could any regulation have ever have stopped such a determined and essentially well respected man?

There are probably other scams going on today in the financial markets that may never be discovered, but some will come to light one day. No amount of regulation, monitoring, observation and reporting will ever reveal the determined fraudster. As with the gambler who needs their kicks, they will do anything to get the adrenalin rush.

Before you get too hot under the collar, most of us are participating in the biggest Ponzi scheme going and it is entirely legal. It is called the State Benefit System. Take state pensions, as an example. Whilst working you pay into a scheme some of your money. This money is not invested for you, but it is recorded as a payment that you have made. It is allocated for your future benefit, but the money that you have paid into the scheme is immediately used to pay the equivalent of client A in a Ponzi scheme, i.e. those who have already retired. When you retire, as client B, you require client C to continue to pay into the Ponzi scheme.

This has all the trade marks of a Ponzi scheme. If you do your sums, there ain't enough going into the scheme to be a sustainable scheme long term. The only way of sustaining the scheme is through one of several things:

1. Vastly higher rates of taxation;
2. Reduce the returns (benefits) for investors;
3. Borrow more money—worry about how to repay this another day;
4. Extend—significantly—the retirement age;
5. End the scheme.

Go on you choose, option 1, 2, 3, 4 or 5. Politically no party is ever going to choose option 5, they would never be re-elected. But there will be some sort of sputtering death in this scheme, somewhere, someday, just like any Ponzi scheme. There are three possible outcomes to any Ponzi scheme, and three only:

1. The promoter (the government) will vanish (not be re-elected), taking all of the remaining investors (taxpayers) money (the state benefits) with them (any new government will cut benefits—drastically).
2. The scheme will begin to collapse under its own weight as the investment (that is the taxes that are being collected) slows and the promoter (the government) starts having problems paying the promised returns (state benefits).
3. External market forces, such as a sharp decline in the economy will cause many investors (taxpayers) to withdraw part or all of their funds (become unemployed, or the wealthy will leave the country due to high taxation), simply due to underlying market movements.

Thus far I have not used my arbitrator in this chapter, but we are really getting to the core of the human heart. It does not matter whether it be an arable farmer or a livestock farmer near the beginning of the age; or whether it is an immigrant in the 1800s desperate to make money; or a modern day respected investment guru; the human condition is the same, it rarely has the capacity to change without divine purpose and intervention. We have moved our eyes from looking upwards, as Abel did, to that of looking downwards, as Cain did, and when our eyes are diverted we see one anothers wealth and fortune and we fall into the trap of making comparisons. We can also become jealous, or angry at apparent levels of injustice that others have wealth and we have little in comparison. The city wishes to maintain the capitalist economic mantra that wealth is good and inequality is a requirement of capitalism.

Whether any change in the current bonus structures will reduce the likelihood of risk and potential fraud is very much open to question.

CHAPTER TEN

THE FIGHT BACK

Thomas Jefferson is said to have penned the following:
> I sincerely believe…that banking establishments are more dangerous than standing armies, and that the principle of spending money to be paid by posterity under the name of funding is but swindling futurity on a large scale.

The Spanish philosopher George Santayana once wrote:
> Those who cannot remember the past, are condemned to repeat it.

How little we have learned, and how prophetic the words of both Jefferson and Santayana have proved to be. Compare the graphs of the 2008 Chinese Crash; the 2000 technology sector crash; the 1990 Japanese Crash; the 1929 Wall Street Crash. When they are all plotted out they are markedly similar.[xxx] In all of them there is a growth that is extremely rapid, the peak is arrived at, then comes the sharp decline. The technical details as to why each peak and crash came about might differ, but it is a reflection of mankind who is willing to blindly follow the trend, time and time again.

Let's think about this history in a little more detail. How about starting with the following report:

> It was very quiet on last Wednesday on Wall Street, until relatively late in the day when some leading stocks lost value. Most believed this to be a blip on the horizon. During the next few days it became apparent that a weakened president, un-regulated credit markets, combined with investor greed had all begun to take their full toll on share prices. After years of unprecedented growth, the markets fell sharply, by more than 6% on Thursday.
>
> The economic woes of the U.S. began to affect the British market. The

---

[xxx] You can see these charts at: http://www.moneyweek.com/investments/stock-markets/money-morning-stockmarket-crashes-01110.aspx

Labour government tried to take up a leadership position in Europe, but with little real success. Shares in the U.S. continued to plummet. The world stood on the edge of a massive recession.

When do you think this was written? 2008, 2009? The 1990s, or the 1980s? In reality the events referred to in this report happened around 80 years ago. The weakened U.S. President is not Obama, or Bush, but Herbert Hoover. The British Labour government of the time was not headed by the previous premier, Gordon Brown, but Ramsay MacDonald. The similarities between the October 1929 and October 2008 are astounding.

For the small investor the 1929 crash is best reflected in terms of how investments fared. An investment in 1929 that was valued at $10,000 had reduced to about $1,100 by 1932. This is a loss of almost 90%! When the crash of this era is mentioned images of dramatic declines and people jumping out of high rise blocks might spring to mind. In part this was true as the Dow Index dropped by almost 50% in just over two months. However, the decline was far from over so quickly. The markets continued to decline for another two and a half years. So what caused this rapid decline after six solid years of growth? The truth is that no one really knows. What is acknowledged is that we must go back to 1919 to understand the start of this boom.

In post war America there began a boom that was not simulated in financially crippled Europe. The roaring twenties was about to begin.

Firstly, in order to finance the cost of entering into the war—and post WWI—the U.S. government issued Liberty Bonds whereby the government guaranteed a return on these investments. Even the movie stars Charlie Chaplin and Douglas Fairbanks were recruited in the marketing campaign to sell these to the public. Investors willingly took up the option of buying into these cast iron investments.

A new investor had also risen up as a consequence of the world conflict. Many women had learned how to be independent, many had gone out to work and gained a wage. The consequence, women started to become financially independent. They began to make financial decisions and take up the reins of control. These independent minded women, and other first time investors, saw the Liberty Bond as quite an exotic form of investment. It was not much of a leap to move from this and into investing in corporate bonds and other stocks. The perception of safety became blurred quite quickly, especially as the stock market began to rise. It seemed that you could not lose.

A new way of investing also evolved. You did not require the full amount to invest in a stock as you could easily borrow the money. If you wanted to buy some stocks, no problem, you just borrowed the money from your broker. To buy $100,000 of stock you needed as little as $10,000. The broker would loan the remaining $90,000. This was (and is) called buying on "margin".

Stocks were rising rapidly in value, a cheap line of credit to invest was easy to obtain.

It has been commented that Groucho Marx asked his broker how stocks could just continue rising with no downside. To the comedian it just did not make sense. Any such questions were put to one side. Allegedly his broker said to him:

It's different this time it's a global economy.

Does this sound familiar?

On the inside of Wall Street the situation was very different. At the time the city consisted of a small clique. This made insider dealing easy. Brokers would buy stocks from one another at artificially high prices, selling when they had made profits.

New technology also made the buying and selling of stock easier. Ticker tape machines transmitted information across the trading floor more quickly than ever before. By today's standards this was slow, as information on trades could take several hours, especially when under pressure and when trading reached its peak.

Eventually 40 cents in every $1 borrowed in the U.S. was borrowed in order to invest into the stock market. This was a staggering 40% of personal borrowing in the U.S. in order to enable people to buy at "margin"! Borrowing was too high, it was unsustainable. Any bells of familiarity ringing loudly yet? Still investors clamoured to invest in this seemingly never ending bull market. President Coolidge proudly said:

> The business of America is business.

There was next to no regulation in the markets. Again, ring any bells? In contrast to the optimism of the President one commentator said:

> It was a gambling casino that was rigged.

Prior to the crash of 1929, Herbet Hoover had taken up the role of President. Privately Hoover is worried. But, as a politician he does not have the courage of his own convictions and he fails to introduce regulation to curb the excesses. He has no appetite to take on the city and impose tough regulation.

But there was an end to this gravy train of growth. When the markets collapsed, on what has become known as Black Thursday, thousands came to Wall Street. The crowds stood there in silence, dumbstruck having heard the news that stocks were falling and falling fast.

The wealthy and the good called an emergency meeting on Wall Street and some of the richest men in the U.S. came up with a plan. They pooled hundreds of thousands of dollars of their own money and they began to buy stocks at inflated prices, hoping to prop up the market and avoid total collapse.

For a while this strategy worked. But the new technology began to fail. The ticker tape fell behind the trades. The ticker tape machine operators slept on the trading floors after the markets had closed, exhausted and burnt out. As the trading became more frenetic they simply could not keep up. Investors began to discover the risks of buying on "margin". They literally lost everything. Their stocks became worthless but their loans remained outstanding. Borrowing with a variable priced asset being the means of repayment now showed up to being the flawed strategy that it was, and is. Again I must reiterate, are the bells ringing?

By the Tuesday following, cries of sell, sell, sell echoed around the trading floors. Due to the sheer volume of sales the Bankers were swamped. Even they could not intervene. They did not have sufficient funds.

$25 billion of personal wealth of Americans had disappeared in just 5 days!

Banks who had loaned irresponsibly, and loaned big, were now in trouble. Need I say it again, the whacking big bells of recognition must now be ringing loudly. The U.S. stockmarket continued to decline, the ripple effect around the world was devastating.

By 1931 around two thousand banks throughout America had closed taking their savers money with them. Money became tight. Companies with good order books could not gain the required levels of credit as the banks were extremely reluctant to lend. Bells again, anyone? Companies closed and workers were laid off.

Economists are divided as to whether the crash in 1929 caused the Great Depression. It may not have been the sole cause, but it must have been a contributory factor.

When Roosevelt became President he carried out a full investigation into the abuses of the past and he bought in long overdue tougher regulation.

Does any of this resonate with today? Unchecked growth; greed of the city; greed of investors; an expectation for markets to always rise; pledges of politicians to abolish boom and bust; tougher regulation being required, and introduced—post crash; banks lending irresponsibly; banks then being over-cautious in lending etc…

Have we learned anything from the past? Or are we like the philosopher implies, slow learners?

Let's now fast-forward to today. In order to bring the city financiers viewpoint to the discussion, I have attempted to gain an interview from investment analysts and fund managers—those whom the media would collectively term as Bankers. I am grateful to the two who were willing to accede to my request. I now wish to outline the basics of an interview that I held with them.

Derek has been working in the city for several years, more years than he cares to mention, and his colleague John for perhaps a couple of years or so in his current role. They are both fascinating characters. I could engage with them both for many hours. What follows is an abridged version of my brief interview with both of them.

I kicked off by asking Derek about some of the history and how we got to the point of such drama. His considered reply was as follows:

> People saw an opportunity. They found out that it wasn't illegal to create wealth beyond their wildest dreams.
>
> The stock exchange through the 1980s was used for one purpose, to invest the wealth of clients—that is individuals, charities, corporations—for a future dividend income.
>
> As time went on, fewer investors invested for the long term. They were only concerned with the immediate and the short term returns.
>
> Take the trading desks, their sole job is to make money and to make money each day.

Earlier in this book I have outlined how this desire for immediate wealth has become prevalent. We have a desire for the instantaneous. In the story of Nick Leeson, and many others, we can see that pressure has been placed upon workers in the city to produce, and produce fast. This satisfies the bosses of the largest of the financial institutions, but it also satisfies us, the investors. Often we are not prepared to wait for a sustained investment return. Derek continues along a similar theme:

> This is not a new problem, the speed with which the markets can react today may be different, the volume of trades might have increased, but modern technology brings immediacy and the world to our doorstep.
>
> Money for money's sake is not a new concept, as enough is never enough, and this has always been the case. There is an aspiration to acquire more money, a desire to make more than can be imagined.

Trading worldwide has always taken place. For example the silk and spice routes of the East are ancient. In the not too distant past Clive of India sent out an agent to source the manufacture and import of many goods and materials. These goods would be loaded onto ships, they would be sailed half way around the world. This whole process took time.

The difference between the ships of an age gone by and today is twofold. Firstly the number of hands that these commodities and goods now pass through has increased markedly; secondly the speed in which they are valued is so much quicker. The world's markets can receive news more quickly due to the global communications network that is at our disposal.

When I started working in the city—arbitraging Gold—it took several months, but today's process is far quicker. Even employment opportunities are on a global scale.

But you cannot tell me that the basics involved are any different. For instance, when a tea clipper was coming into the docks in Chatham, there must have been someone standing on the docks guessing the amount of tea that was on board the ship by assessing how low in the water the ship was sitting. They would then assume a price for the load, trying to sell it before the ship was docked whilst hoping to buy it back, once unloaded, for a healthy profit.

Derek's point is a good one. Trading has been going on in one form or another, since time immemorial. The trading markets of every major city in the world are simply a derivation of something that is as ancient as the hills.

I continued by asking Derek what he thinks has gone wrong? As always, his reply is telling:

The city got it very wrong. The culture that grew up was one of: exposure = importance. (A wry smile has formed upon John's face.)

By this, I mean that brokers and traders, believed that if they took a risk—sometimes with complexity—they were somehow important, almost indispensable.

This goes back to the aim of the city who wanted to create money, on a daily basis, but underneath the capital asset value of these investments was extremely weak.

You can blame anyone for this, but it is more basic; it is this underlying aspiration to have more. The likes of Scott Mead created money, but nothing that he created was of any real intrinsic capital value.

Derek is right. The value that we place upon things in life are a direct result of meeting a demand. For example, a building that shelters us from the rain and the cold, is what we would term as a basic need; if the shelter is simply a few walls with a simple roof, it may have little monetary value, but it is of huge physical importance. Transport the house to containing many rooms to sleep in, eat in, to wash and bathe in, the monetary value of the building will increase. Transport the same building into the countryside, perhaps into a pretty hamlet or village, in the South-East of the country, it will acquire even more monetary value. We have lost the art of valuing the importance of the basic necessity of a house that protects us from the elements. We have made this basic necessity of our lives into something far more than it need be as we value houses in monetary terms, rather than being an asset that protects us.

We also have fast food chains that have now become so prevalent because we bought into the concept of satisfying our physical hunger now.

Car manufacturers produced bigger, better and faster cars with more electric windows and with a sunroof, because we were prepared to buy into them, not because transport was essential to us, but it is the manner in which we wanted to be transported that became, and has become, important to many of us, me included.

I am not laying the blame for the economic downturn solely at the door of society but it is a contributory factor, as trading in any commodity or asset only takes place when there is a demand for that commodity or asset. As I have said, there is a need for the traders to trade honestly, and not recklessly, for this lack of responsibility by the large institutions is partly to blame for the current crisis, but as I have already said, and I will continue to say, we are in this together and none of us are exempt from blame.

Derek then went on to illustrate the point of reckless behaviour within the city with the following tale:

> There is an investment bank, I have not been able to find out which one yet, but it is said that they are effectively saying, work for us and if you give your bonus to us as collateral, then we will give you shares—in our company—and in the future we will return the collateral to you when you redeem the shares.

This is really no different to buying on "margin" in the 1920s. It is a stupid practice! Share prices move all of the time and there is no certainty of a return of the capital invested. To give your employer cash and in return accept an asset that fluctuates wildly in value, in a company that has little of an intrinsic capital value is utterly absurd. Yet these same people are being trusted with our investments! The question is what happens when things go wrong? How will the firm redeem the shares for cash then? This highlights the extremely flawed nature of some in the city.

I moved on by asking Derek and John if any lessons have been learned. I asked them as to how close to the edge of the precipice we might be? Derek gave the following reply:

> Some lessons have been learned and some things are slowly changing, like the criteria for lending. We have stepped back a long way from the cliff edge, but we are not safe yet, and we never really will be 100% safe, but we do still need to move further back. There are still some problems and these problems are yet to be overcome.
>
> A dangerous phrase that is now kicking around is that, it's different this time. After all that has happened this is a naive and disappointing attitude. Whether lessons have really been learned, I don't really know. Only time will tell.
>
> And conversely on the radar now there is also the phrase: I can't do that because I don't know if it will work or not.

The city—and the world's markets—are now caught between these two principles. First, some say, it cannot happen again, as the Titanic cannot sink a second time! I agree with Derek that this is a rather arrogant and rather worrying attitude. Any who think this have learned little from this recent crisis, the crash in 1929 and all of the downturns in the markets, ever! The second concept of I can't risk it a second time, causes some to become paralysed by fear. Such paralysis will inhibit their investment decisions which, by their very nature, contains some element of risk. Both of these positions are unhealthy. I wonder what happens next time—for there will be a next time? John considers this and he responds with refreshing honesty:

> The truth. No one knows. All I can say is that we are survivors.

Derek takes up this theme.

> I would also say that it is a game. This game that we are playing has no end point. We may all want different things from the game, but it is still a game nevertheless. The game is competitive, but you must be honest when you play it.
>
> No one will ever win the game, that is impossible as the game never ends, but some will have a better and more complete game plan than the rest of the players. There are also many variations in the game. This means that there is a potential for more failures. Because the game is now on a global scale the failures can be spectacular, but so can the returns.

I agree that this investing lark can be likened to a game, it can also have devastating and far reaching consequences whether we get it wrong, or right. But, when playing a board game such as Monopoly, no one is hurt, but when a financier is risking your life's savings in this game, that is far more serious. Working in the city Derek is one of the good guys, as is his colleague, John. They are both trying their best. They act honestly, sometimes they win, and then, so do their clients. But sometimes they lose, and then, so will their clients (materially speaking). We need to understand this as we invest. We need to learn to understand the risks and the limitations of the game.

On the issue of the blame game, Derek calmly voices his opinion:

> Some of what the media have said and written is justified, some is also hype. I wonder whether these critics if they had had the same opportunity would have done anything that differently. (John nods his head in agreement.)
>
> Generally people started to ignore long term aims on their investments. They started to turn away from investing in physical assets; and investors and managers alike stopped analysing what they were investing in.
>
> The consequences of this failure is a lashing out and the need to blame someone.
>
> This desire for wealth and status is also reflected in society. You just have to look at the celebrity culture and all of the reality TV that bombards our screens.
>
> I remember seeing someone winning Big Brother and when they came out of the Big Brother house they were asked what they would do next. Their reply was marked. They said:
>
> > Oh, I think I will go and do Celebrity Big Brother.

Why did this nobody now assume that they had earned a right to be called a celebrity?

Again this is a reflection of what some in the city believed (as I have mentioned previously), exposure = importance! We all like (or even need) warm strokes and we might enjoy praise and acknowledgement, in itself there might be nothing wrong in this, but it is when we come to the place of believing in our own publicity, this has the potential to create an arrogant being within all of us.

At the beginning of my interview with Derek and John, I kicked off with what they thought had gone wrong. Derek's reply was enlightening:

> Do you want the detailed answer, or the quick version? He paused and then he said: The short answer is moral ineptitude.

Though Derek approaches matters from a different position of faith and philosophical background (it is unlikely that he will agree with all that I have written) he and I do agree on many issues regarding motivation for investing and that many of us have lost our way somewhat.

Whether greater regulation and a far tougher approach will achieve anything new, I doubt it. There will always be the extreme risk taker, somewhere, in some office of a big banking institution. Inevitably there will still be the fraudster building a scheme such as one that is based upon the principles of Ponzi.

Derek has about summed it up quite neatly, for once again, we have gone in a complete circle. We return to the state and the condition of the fallen human heart. In my following conclusion this fallen state is ever more apparent.

CHAPTER ELEVEN

HERE ENDETH TODAY'S LESSON

Someone has recently won £113,000,000 on a lottery! Wow. This is a record-breaking sum won from the Euro-Millions draw. This will make the winner the 586th wealthiest person in Britain, overnight. They will be richer than Jamie Oliver, Cheryl Cole and John Terry combined! This is what you call loaded! But there is another underlying story behind this win. The real winner took quite a while to claim this prize. A spokesman for the organisers of the draw, Camelot, said:

> Over 1,000 people or syndicates contacted us this time hoping it was them. Some said they had matched the numbers but couldn't find their ticket but a lot of them said they didn't think it was them, but they just wanted to check just in case.
>
> A lot of people who do a lucky dip will be unsure what numbers they had, so if they can't find their ticket they feel they have to put their mind at rest, they can't live with the idea that it could be them.

Without doubting the sincerity, or the word, of these good people who claimed this prize, can you really believe that all of these 1,000 were genuinely mistaken? I doubt it. There was one lady who rang in insisting that she had noted down the winning numbers on a notepad, but her husband had lost the ticket, apparently. This is a frequent habit of her husband's, the losing of her tickets. The question in my mind is simple; why does this lady continue to give her weekly lottery ticket to her husband for safe-keeping, when he misplaces it so often? Her reasoning, along with her actions, makes no sense.

This incident helps to illustrate how the popular mainstream media can be gripped with such a consuming intensity over this lottery win, and over wealth in general. People wanted to know who had won such a large amount of money. It also shows that some of the claimants were either—at best—mistaken, or they were calculating liars. The remaining alternative is that they were deluded as they genuinely convinced themselves that they had indeed won this fortune.

The pursuit of wealth is often seen as a route to happiness, by many, but surely this unhealthy pastime has been a major contributory factor in the crisis that currently faces us, for it has affected the manner in which we perceive the essentials of our lives.

As part of BBC Radio 3's Free Thinking Festival a survey on happiness was conducted. Half of the people surveyed said that more cash would make them happier overnight. A staggering 88% said that a lottery win would make them happy. When the 2,000 respondents were asked what caused unhappiness, 65% said that it was the state of their finances. Interestingly spending time with the family was only chosen as the number one route to happiness by just 9%. Abigail Appleton, head of speech programmes at BBC Radio 3 said:

It's fascinating that money is still prevalent in pursuing happiness.

I'm with Abigail on this, but I would go even further. It is sad that most of those polled placed wealth above that of their relationships with family. And if family will not make us happy, what of our stuff, how does that fare?

Earlier I commented upon our thought process and the manner in which we have replaced the physical necessity of having a home with a more materialistic perception of a home being an asset with an inherent value and that we have done a similar thing with attitudes to the even more basic commodities of food and drink. An entire TV industry has grown up around the concept of making food more tasty and attractive—at times it is made into something that is incredibly too fancy for my liking. A whole dietary industry has also bloomed.

It is the same with clothes. We need our garments to protect us from the elements, it is as basic as that. To make our feet comfortable, for example, we encase them in leather or canvas. Yet what has become of importance to us are the labels. Is what I wear designer? (My mother used to tuck my label inside my jumper, now we wear the labels on the outside of our clothes in order to make a statement about our wealth.) This point is more than ably illustrated by the (very funny in my view) comedian Peter Kay in his autobiography entitled The Sound of Laughter where he relates the following tale:

> I only succumbed to materialistic temptation once. I had to go to the optician's. I wasn't keen on going as the last thing I needed in my un-cool life was a spazzy pair of National Health glasses, but my mum insisted...While we were walking back from the optician's, we passed a local sports shop and I fell in love with a pair of Nike trainers in the window.
>
> They were white and when I say white I mean blinding white. The golden rule in '87 was the whiter the trainer, the cooler you were. My mum bought them for me...I went back to school in the afternoon...I strolled down the road and through the school [gates] like John Travolta in *Saturday Night Fever*.
>
> There were a few stares and mumbles as I walked by but I didn't care. It was a beautiful summer's day. There just wasn't a cloud in the blue sky above me and I was cool just for once in my life. I got to class and before I could sit down Big Mouth Gareth Riley decided to [make fun of me].
>
> 'Hello Kay, I like your new Nick trainers.'
>
> A few stifled laughs followed.
>
> 'If you open your eyes smart-arse you'll actually see they're Nike,' I replied smugly.
>
> 'No they're not, they're Nick's.'
>
> He said it so indignantly that I had no choice but to casually glance down and read them...He was right. They were Nick trainers, a...poor copy of Nike for...poor people who couldn't read.

Peter Kay, as a school child, had a desire for the designer brand. Imagine the smirks and the laughter at his Nick brand of trainers. He also says that he has only succumbed to a materialistic impulse just this one time. If this is the case—and I have no reason to disbelieve this statement—then he is a better man than me, by far as he is certainly ahead of me in this aspect of materialism within our respective spiritual paths.

As I have said, there is nothing wrong with wealth, (there is also nothing wrong with fine food and wine), but by replacing the physical necessity of nourishment with a Michelin star, or two, that might dictate where we eat, or by replacing the need to be in garments that give us warmth, with the apparently necessary designer label, is a distortion of values. I do not believe that this is how we were created to be. We were created in a paradise of sheer beauty and generosity, by a generous God and then we blew it. When mankind was created there is one amazing fact. Read with me in Genesis Chapter 2:

> [25] The man and his wife were both naked, and they felt no shame.

In this verse we read of the man and the woman, standing there, in front of one another, yet they felt no embarrassment. I read this as meaning that they felt totally and utterly comfortable in one another's presence. This is how we were meant to live, forever, in union with God. But, when mankind succumbed and ate of the forbidden fruit, what was the first thing they did. In the third Chapter of this creation story we read:

> [6] When the woman saw that the fruit of the [forbidden] tree was good for food and pleasing to the eye, and also desirable for gaining wisdom, she took some and ate it. She also gave some to her husband, who was with her, and he ate it. [7] Then the eyes of both of them were opened, and they realised they were naked; so they sewed fig leaves together and made coverings for themselves. [8] Then the man and his wife heard the sound of the LORD God as he was walking in the garden in the cool of the day, and they hid from the LORD God among the trees of the garden.

The fruit on the tree looked like good food, we are told. This fruit might be good to taste, but to partake of it held consequences. When the knowledge came upon them they felt the shame. They entered into a sinful state. (I have not the time or space to enter into the theology on sex and that sex and the human form is not dirty—that is for another time.) When they gained knowledge they became aware of sin and they covered themselves. They experienced shame for they could not handle the knowledge that they had acquired.

So it is with wealth—whether this be in a monetary form, or any other—it looks so good, for it is very pleasing on the eye, but to handle it, like the fruit of the tree of knowledge, it is hard, very hard. There is a temptation to be led astray as we bite into the fruit of wealth. We will begin to forget a God of provision, instead we lust after the fruit on the 'wealth' tree. This is what has happened in many parts of the world of finance. The Bankers, like my friend Derek has commented, that the market traders and the financiers have gone down the route of "moral ineptitude" as well as becoming far to concentrated upon profits. Once they have entered this cul-de-sac then the tree of wealth becomes the unobtainable dream. Like the tree of knowledge, once tasted you will always want to come back for more. Enough, as we have discovered, will never be enough.

I believe that when the human heart turns away from our heavenly creator God, who is generous beyond measure, and when, like Cain, we start to look at the offerings and willing heart of others; or when we start to look at the wealth of the likes of Lord Sugar, Bill Gates and even ex-politicians such as Tony Blair, we will sometimes feel jealousy rise up within us.

Like Cain, who looked at self and his own produce we are at the same place. We can tend to view success in our career—however you may term success—as being down to my ability; my energy; my attitudes; my willingness; my long hours worked; my sacrifice; my knowledge; my training; my aptitude. How many 'mys' is that? We have divorced self, our aspirations and work ethic from God. Even if we have a faith, we can fall into the trap of seeing work as being for the week and faith is for Sundays, or when we are gathered in a holy huddle. One Rabbi Meir says that:

> One should teach his son a clean, easy trade and pray to Hashem, for wealth or poverty do not result from the trade, rather, from merit.

This teaching resounds of several things, some I agree with, some I do not. The requisite to teach an easy and clean trade, these I do not agree with, but I do agree that wealth and poverty is the result of merit, or effort and application.

Once we have finished what we deem to be our working life we look forward to retirement. Where in the Holy Bible is retirement mentioned? Rest is there as a command, but nowhere is an extended number of years and the relinquishing of work mentioned in the Holy Bible. Work is also there from the beginning. Take a look at the second account of the creation in the Bible in Genesis, Chapter 2 and verse 5:

> …no shrub of the field had yet appeared on the earth and no plant of the field had yet sprung up, for the Lord God had not sent rain on the earth and there was no man to work the ground…

It appears that there is an order here. God has created the earth and the creation requires someone to work with it. Often we are taught that work is a consequence of sin. This is wrong. A curse is placed upon the beauty of the created order and the created order suffers due to the sin of mankind as this sin brings a curse, but the original order is not flawed. This condemnation, or curse, is highlighted in Genesis, Chapter 3 when God says:

> [17b]"Cursed is the ground because of you;
> through painful toil you will eat food from it
> all the days of your life.
> [18]It will produce thorns and thistles for you,
> and you will eat the plants of the field.
> [19]By the sweat of your brow
> you will eat your food
> until you return to the ground,
> since from it you were taken;
> for dust you are and to dust you will return."

We need to redefine what work is. I don't believe that work is solely about making profits. It is not about wealth gathering. For advisers like myself, and for the so called Bankers who claim that they are doing the will of God, and for all of us, work needs to be re-defined as doing the best for the client. In spiritual terms it is honouring God on a daily basis. For future generations we need to pass on this rediscovery of truth. I like the teaching of one Rabbi Yehudah who says:

> Anyone who does not teach his son a trade, [it is as if] he teaches him robbery.

Personally I believe that we need a moral compass outside that of the one that has been manufactured by man. We need an impartial judge. I believe that the scriptures of the Holy Bible are it. Like the learned Rabbi holy scriptures declare in Proverbs, Chapter 22 and verse 6 that we should:

> Train a child in the way he should go, and when he is old he will not turn from it.

There has been something missing from the moral compass of the financial institutions and trading arenas. They have lost and forgotten the training of their childhood, or it is more likely that it was not there in the first place. Many have no impartial moral reference point, they continue to worship the concept of wealth instead of a creator God being the starting point.

Bankers have turned to placing too much store upon the valuing profits on an all too frequent daily basis. City financiers now look to ways of meeting the heavy demands and impositions of their bosses through this concentration upon profits, for profits sake. The markets will inevitably become more risky (again) and full of complex products that few can understand if this concentration continues. Institutions will fail again and there will be high rolling fraudsters investing on our behalf who are no better than a card sharp. There will also be those, of faith, or no faith, who have grasped the concept of doing the best for their clients rather than for their own pockets.

I believe that man has learned little from the likes of Ponzi. As we have seen, the state of the markets today is very similar to those of 1929. The mechanism that has caused the various crashes may be different, but the reason for the current economic down turn and that of 1929 is—I maintain—the same. It is one of greed, nothing more, nothing less.

I also believe that there will be other crashes. They will probably be even more spectacular than anything we have seen thus far. I do not believe that we are out of the mire, I do not think that we are even at the eye of the storm yet. The governments of the world only have pockets that are so deep. With the massive increases in the cost of welfare provision on the horizon, I do not believe that the government of the U.K. (and most governments of the world) could withstand another cataclysmic crash of the like that we have just seen. This current bail out is barely affordable. If another downturn occurred I believe that some banks and institutions would have to be allowed to go bust.

For people to declare that it is different this time, is pure folly. It is not different, and it will never be different until the condition of the human heart is transformed. We can throw as much technology at the problem combined with a new raft of regulations, but the determined fraudster, such as the once respected Madoff or Leeson, will always be able to find a way around the rules. To believe that the rules and regulations of mankind are capable of ruling the corrupt heart of man is also folly. If someone believes that they can get away with it then they will give it a bash, irrelevant of the toughness of the watchdog.

If the trading desks fail to acknowledge that the money they are investing is their clients hard earned money, then they will continue to take unnecessary risks with our pensions and investments, which will lead to dramatic trends, both up and down, in the global markets.

While the likes of Jot continue to see wealthy bosses earning seven figures salaries, when they earn little in comparison; and when they have an opportunity to rob others, they might take the chance to do so.

If politicians continue to lend to fellow governments many, many billions, without fully checking out the financial stability of the country to whom they are lending and if they fail to pass even a cursory glance over the balance sheet of such countries and their ability to repay these huge debts, the world's markets will continue to live on a knife edge. (To understand this a little more you should watch the video by the Australian comedy duo Clarke and Dawe. It is very, very funny, and it would be even funnier if it weren't so true and so it is worrying.[xxxi]) This knife edge existence is more apparent today as the European governments are now throwing money at the problem economies of the PIGS. (This is the common and apparently affectionate phrase that has recently arisen. It is not meant to be derogatory to the people of Portugal, Ireland, Greece and Spain). Billions are being thrown at Ireland. It is reckoned that Portugal is next, but the one that everyone is petrified of is Spain. Collapse there will bring austerity and devastation. Quite how much no one knows.

Whilst we hunger for ever larger houses, accompanied by ever larger mortgage debt; whilst we fail to acknowledge the generous provision of our heavenly God and whilst we give a high materialistic value to commodities that are of a physical necessity, we will never have enough. There will always be more to taste and partake of at the 'wealth' tree. An even bigger house; a bigger and better car; another set of clothes; a better pair of designer glasses to help us to look cool; or a Rolex to wear upon our wrist.

Whilst we continue to allow the largest Western democracy to repossess the houses of the unfortunate; and in the U.K., if we continue to stand silent as house after house is repossessed and accept that the dispossessed are deemed to have made themselves voluntarily homeless; then we will continue to walk down the very painful road of injustice.

If the prophets remain silent and fail in their duty to speak out. And if they fail to correct the politicians by sticking their necks on the line, and if they fail to become a coherent voice for the poor, injustice will inevitably continue and it will be down to the likes of charities such as Credit Action and CAP to rescue the poor, the downtrodden and those who have fallen upon hard times. The church needs to wake from its slumber and get behind the likes of these organisations and they need to think of how their own church can reflect the Biblical messages of life within their own structures. I guarantee that debt relief organisations and faith communities

---

[xxxi] You can see this video at: http://www.creditwritedowns.com/2010/05/clarke-and-dawes-european-lending-merry-go-round.html

will be required even more, one day. Charles Dickens, the Victorian author and commentator said:

No one is useless in this world who lightens the burdens of another.

This country will need a people to lighten the load of many in such a drastic manner one day. That day might be soon upon us.

Economists say that the levels of personal debt in the U.K. (and other mainstream countries) is affordable and under control. But the rules of economics have been torn up. For example, I have not yet heard a consensus of opinion from the economists and financiers as to what will cause interest rates to increase. We think and assume that they will increase, but when, under what circumstances and by how much, that is the elusive question? I will not go into an economic discussion here, but suffice it to say that the rules of yesterday are gone. They are dead and buried, but they may, like the Phoenix, rise from the ashes. Policy makers are now in the position of having to guess at what resolutions will work.

If we continue to believe that social benefits are ours by right and not the privilege of a developed and just world; and if we expect the welfare state to remain in its current form, the National Debt will continue to rise well beyond the current unsustainable levels. Politicians will always want to be re-elected and cutting down on the welfare state sufficiently is an unlikely vote winner.

I believe that our God in heaven is literally crying over the condition of the human heart. Our hearts need to turn away from the transitory wealth of this world and back heavenward, to our glorious God and his riches that have no monetary value. We need to call out once again for his mercy. The riches on offer from our God have a value beyond anything on this God-given earth. I don't believe that God wants us to continue to live and work in an environment of fear, jealousy, pride, arrogance, superiority and judgementalism. We desperately need to transform our lives and our hearts. We need to re-discover the reality of establishing this heaven upon the earth. Yeshua (Jesus) taught us these essentials in a prayer when he said:

[9]"This, then, is how you should pray:

> " 'Our Father in heaven,
> hallowed be your name,
> ¹⁰your kingdom come,
> your will be done
> on earth as it is in heaven…

These are a few lines from the most prayed prayer of all. We are to pray for this glorious kingdom of HIS to come, here and now, on this earth! This is a kingdom that has no war, no conflict, no suffering, no poverty, no injustice, no sickness and—so very importantly—in heaven there is absolutely no money and no stuff! Imagine that, a world with no money. This is radical teaching folks. While we continue to live on earth there will always be a need for food, clothes and so on, and we will still be stewards, until we ascend into heaven. But essentially we need to break out and imagine what this would be like if we relied upon the provision of a just God, sharing all that we have been given, with one another, so that none is in need.

We may overcome the current crisis as clever economists, and politicians—who really do need our prayers at this time—devise a man made rescue plan that will dig us out of the mess that we are in, for a while at least. But we need more than these man made, ill thought structures, rules and regulations. God offers us so much more through his discipline of ultimate love. This is not just an ancient tale, the Biblical accounts are not just for kids at Christmas, they are a reality, embedded in humanity and they are as real today as ever they were. I firmly believe that God wants us to begin to experience this reality today, here and now.

So how do we begin to clamber back up the economic ladder? Until a new kingdom is heralded and ushered in, we need wealth producers and city workers for the sake of our man made institutions. But we need to look at how we can carry out wealth production in a fair, just and equitable manner, with the aim of eliminating poverty and the raft of debt that is currently crippling society.

Many have commented upon what is required. We have learned that the government—no matter their political hue—are facing desperate times that call for desperate measures, but over all of the talk and decision making there needs to be mercy and grace.

When I look ever closer at the teaching of Rabbi Yeshua, this first century Palestinian itinerant preacher, I see the breath of grace. He showed us that if we live by and through a power upon high, then there are no rules. The rules of the ten commandments were put up as boundaries, but if we were living in union with God, then there would be no need for boundaries, regulations and laws, for we would be living in accordance with his divine purpose. Who needs rules if you have something better? To many this concept is ethereal and some kind of away with the fairies teaching, even something to be mocked and scorned. Everyone is entitled to their opinion, but during the last Labour government, they passed more new criminal laws than any government before them. I once read that they had passed more laws than all governments combined in the U.K. since the end of WWII! I ask this question. Has this frenzied law making made any real difference? For example, because someone can go to prison for failing to have a horn or bell upon their bicycle, has this draconian law bought a real significant change to the quality of our lives? Apparently—I once read—it is also now illegal to sell grey squirrels door to door![xxxii] I am being flippant, but it does beg the question: which would you prefer, an investment manager investing according to heavenly principles, or an investment manager investing according to both politically and bonus motivated principles?

I hope that you can see that I have attempted to be fair in my assessment of the causes of this current economic and financial crisis. The difficulties that we have experienced is a collective responsibility. The cure must also be no less than a collective effort, but it would be best if this effort leaned toward the divine kingdom, small step by small step.

At the time of writing the current government has announced the biggest raft of cuts that we have seen for aeons. Is this action right? I don't know. No-one can

---

[xxxii] For the source of this claim, please go to: http://www.dailymail.co.uk/debate/article-1262676/RICHARD-LITTLEJOHN-If-justice-Im-goldfish.html

really tell. In about five to seven years we will be able to assess the situation. At this time the best that we can expect of the government is that they will have the courage and resolve to carry through what they think and believe to be the best for the country. For our part it is time for us to get down on our knees to pray for them.

And of the Bankers and their bonuses, let's stop the blame culture. My arbitrator calls for forgiveness on the one part, and repentance on the other. Continuing to hold a grudge will not solve anything. I firmly believe that there needs to be a fairer distribution of earnings, commissions and bonuses across the financial sector. This is more than apparent, but what has been has happened. No amount of moaning will change history. Praying for the city workers and their employers would be a more beneficial use of our energy and time. I also believe that there needs to be a shrinking in the size of the financial institutions and the banks. A lack of choice inevitably reduces competition and costs go up.

God's kingdom on earth, may appear to be a long way off, but until we hunger for it by turning toward heavenly principles, I believe that there is little hope of redemption through man-made institutions and regulations.

Once this crisis is over—if it ever is—there may be another one to endure. Perhaps the current downturn may yet continue for sometime and it may yet cut even deeper.

In order to restore some semblance of balance we need an arbitrator to guide us. There is no better place to start than the beginning of time itself. As I have said previously, in the creation story there is an order and a balance within the physical environment. There is a purpose to each part of the creation (this has been proven as our scientific knowledge has increased). Of this balanced created order, in the first chapter of Genesis, the account says:

> [31]God saw all that he had made, and it was very good. And there was evening, and there was morning—the sixth day.

This order and balance is described as being "very good". Anything that is this good, must have within it much to admire, for there nothing erroneous within it. But this good and balanced order became distorted by the actions of mankind. When it was pointed out to them what they were missing, a desire to take what was forbidden rose up and they grabbed at the opportunity, hungrily. This is like Jot seeing the opulence around her. She wanted to taste and eat of it.

Through disobedience and rebellion against God by mankind there is a consequence. Our inherited legacy is that our values have become distorted, as I keep saying, enough is never enough.

But one day—thankfully—my arbitrator is clear that all that is transitory will disappear. Our distorted values will once again be realigned and they will come into balance, then we will see that such a kingdom is indeed, "very good" and we will have the opportunity to dwell in that undistorted realm, for eternity. Whilst we continue to see just a glimpse of this kingdom, things will continue to be hard.

If the Bankers—and ourselves—were to take on board just one passage from my arbitrator, I would ask them—and all of us—to look in the book of Deuteronomy, Chapter 8:

> [17]You may say to yourself, "My power and the strength of my hands have produced this wealth for me." [18]But remember the LORD your God, for it is he who gives you the ability to produce wealth, and so confirms his covenant, which he swore to your forefathers, as it is today.

God gives us the ability to produce wealth. But it should not be about us, there can be no pride in our own achievements, for in the coming kingdom, our own ability will be worthless, as will be our riches. So my prayer is that the financial capitals of the world and the workers in the global institutions will begin to transform their hearts and that they will learn from the past as they taste of the fruit of the 'wealth' tree.

I pray that we all might remember that the wealth we benefit from is indeed transitory. More importantly it is our God in heaven who enables us to create such vast levels of wealth and not us and our clever schemes. As Goldman Sachs, Bear Stearns, Lehmann Brothers, A.I.G., Merrill Lynch and so many others have learned, the dreams of man are fatally flawed.

We all need to learn the lesson that a restoration process and a re-alignment of the heart of mankind is long overdue. The original undistorted Eden concept of man living under the protection of—and in union with—God needs to be given the chance to become as much of a reality as it can.

The alternative to this transformation and re-alignment is to depend upon wealth and riches and all that this offers to the human heart. If this is your preferred option, be warned:

> Wealth is like sea water. The more that you drink it, the thirstier you will become.[xxxiii]

[xxxiii] A proverb of the German Philosopher, Arthur Schopenhauer. 1788 - 1860.

AUTHOR'S NOTE

While every effort has been made to ensure that all sources have been correctly referenced and attributed, and that all accounts, dates and times are correct, there is always the possibility of error. If errors of attribution or detail subsequently come to light, they will be rectified in future reprints.

I have also conducted extensive research on many aspects of this book. As with many matters in life, when reviewing past events opinions often differ. Where differences of opinion do exist I have endeavoured to point this out and make a judgement as to what I believe may have caused something to occur, or what has taken place.

There are also many, many other examples of financial institutions that almost, or did collapse, or had to be rescued. I have barely scratched the surface in examining the financial tsunami that has hit the world's economies.

If you wish to do so you can read further on the failure of Lehman Brothers; or how about Merrill Lynch, who became so concerned regarding their own vulnerable position and their likely collapse, they persuaded the Bank of America to acquire the company outright. Regarding government support, what of the U.S. government spending to the tune of $85 billion to bail out one of the world's largest insurers, A.I.G.? In the month following this bail out, the New York Stock Exchange fell by about 25%!

We have faced the most dramatic down-turn, in terms of volume losses at least, in the history of the globe. I do not believe that we have yet seen the conclusion to this episode, it may just be the beginning of a prolonged exposure of the consequences of human greed and lust for power at the expense of the like of you and I. The truth is, no one really knows where, or when it will turn around. There is just the hope that it will. I hope that it will do so, and lessons will be learned and that it will truly be different this time.

On that positive note, I do hope that you have enjoyed reading this book.

Arwyn Bailey.

ACTION POINTS

If you are so inclined here are some suggested prayer points:

- Think about any times that you, your church or anyone you know has been greedy. Say sorry to God.
- Ask God to help you to be willing to do what is right with your money.
- Think about your own debts and those of the country. Ask God to help you, personally, and your country in the handling of debt.
- Say sorry to God for your nations lack of support for the poor.
- Pray that God will give wisdom to the leaders of your nation on how they should deal with the current financial crisis.
- Ask God to stabilise the economies of the world and for a reformation to take place.
- Ask God to establish a sense of righteousness in the markets.
- Pray that God will raise up an economy based upon Biblical principles.
- Pray that the church, including those you belong to or those around you, will become an influence for the good and that they will meet the needs of the poor in these austere times.
- Dare to pray for a revival to break out in the financial markets.
- Ask God to show you how to give to the poor and projects that you can support.
- Consider giving to CAP, Credit Action or Crown Financial Ministries in their quest to release people from debt and to educate in the matters of finance.

  http://www.capuk.org/donate/donate.php

  http://www.creditaction.org.uk/contact.html

  http://www.crown.org/GetInvolved/

USEFUL SITES AND CONTACTS

If you are needing help with any aspect of financial planning, or if you are struggling with debt, here are some websites that you might find useful:

- CAP — http://www.capuk.org/home/index.php
  If you are struggling with debt this is a good starting point. You can check if you can gain access to free debt counselling in your area from this site.

- Credit Action — http://www.creditaction.org.uk/
  A site that is brimming with information on all things financial. Probably the best resources on the internet. The site includes calculators, leaflets and literature to help you, and your church, to understand and manage wealth in a healthy manner.

- Crown Financial Ministries — http://www.crown.org/default.aspx
  A fantastic educational resource on wealth and wealth management.

- http://www.creditaction.org.uk/resources/useful-organisations.html
  As a part of Credit Action's website, this page lists many useful links to other useful sites and organisations including debt advice help-lines and centres.

- ACFA —http://www.christianfinancialadvisers.org.uk/
  The Association of Christian Financial Advisers website. You can check to see if you have a Christian adviser in your area. All advisers who belong to this association are required to sign up to, and adhere to, a code consisting of some ethical and faith based principles.

- AIFA — http://www.aifa.net/consumer-area/ifap.php
  Here you can search for an independent Financial Adviser in your area.

- FSA — http://www.fsa.gov.uk/
  The site of the Financial Services Authority. This is the regulator of most matters pertaining to finance.

SUGGESTED READING

Nevertheless — John Kirkby

The story of CAP (Christians Against Poverty). This is a must read if you wish to know about the real problem of debt today; how people are endeavouring to transform nations; and how lives can be changed.

This book can be obtained, free of charge at:
http://www.capuk.org/involved/nevertheless.php

Your Money and Your Life — Keith Tondeur OBE & Steve Pierce

A practical book that examines the issue of money and how to handle wealth in an honouring manner in order to be free to live life.

Biblical Finance — Mark Lloydbottom

A Biblical reflection on finance, wealth and what this nebulous thing called money, wealth and possessions are.

Your Money Counts — Mark Lloydbottom with Howard Dayton

In the U.K. we are one of the wealthiest nations in the globe. Just how should we honour God with our money, possessions and stuff that we own?

Love Work, Live Life:
Releasing God's Purpose in Work — David Oliver

A practical discourse upon the thing that we have labelled as work, from a Biblical perspective. A must read for anyone, who is at work.

Money, Possessions and Eternity — Randy Alcorn

This is a well researched book that looks at money from a Biblical perspective. It succeeds in shedding light upon many areas of your life. It covers topics such as: saving; investing; pensions; renting versus buying a house. There is also a very good section on teaching children how to use money wisely.

House of Cards:
Tale of Hubris and Wretched Excess on Wall Street — William D. Cohan

This book is an autopsy on what went wrong in order to bring about the demise of Bear Stearns after more than 80 years of trading!

Two Trillion Dollar Meltdown:
Easy Money, High Rollers, and the Great Credit Crash — Charles Morris

This lawyer delves into more of the reasons behind the credit crunch, and why the global crisis has come about. The language is ideal for the lay person.

Great Depression: A Diary — Benjamin Roth

When you read this book you realise that there are many similarities between the crash of 1929 and the current economic crisis. This diary shows that mankind has learned little since these days of economic disaster.

This Time is Different:
Eight Centuries of Financial Folly — C.M. Reinhart & K.S. Rogoff

This book provides a great deal of raw data and empirical observations on the various crises, that economies have experienced over the centuries. It is not overly technical, but it is not a light or easy read. It is a good book to have on your shelf to dip into as and when you like.

The Holy Bible — God (sort of)

This is a bargain as it is 66 books rolled into one. A book that contains answers to some of life's deepest questions whilst the author has retained a great deal of mystery, combined with human stories of financial ineptitude, wealth, sex and innuendo, harems, adultery, deception, brutal murder and destruction, familial conflict, theft, the supernatural exposed, power struggles, humour, love triumphing over evil and a great deal of hope, intertwined with the story of one family tribe over the centuries.

Other important material for further research, understanding and study:

I would recommend almost any book by Keith Tondeur, Mark Lloydbottom and David Oliver, all of whom are leading speakers in the field of business, debt and finance. There is too little room here to list all of their books.

I would also draw your attention to the set of Cambridge Papers that are freely available from the Jubilee Centre. I would particularly recommend those by Paul Mills. This book is not a technical probe into the markets, it is more of a snapshot of the human condition and the emotional roller coaster that we are often faced with. These papers are a far more technical examination than I have entered into and they cover the arena of wealth, the markets and suggestions of how the current systems could be aligned to the ideals of those that we see in the Holy Bible.

You can learn more at: http://www.jubilee-centre.org/topics.php

OTHER BOOKS FROM GALACTIC

At Galactic Publishing we aim to bring to the market, lesser known authors, and unknown authors. Why not try another book co-authored by this author, Noah and the Giraffe.

This is a conversation—in the form of a series of light hearted emails— between a Christian (Arwyn) and an Ignostic (Phil)! Can Arwyn prove the existence of God? Can Phil prove that there is no God? And why does the giraffe have such a long neck? Find out the answer to all of these great questions, and many more.

As a more reflective work, we have published the last work of Myra Chave-Jones, My Swan Song. This book is a reflection upon life's journey by this highly regarded author.

We also have available the new phenomenon, Puzzulti. These are puzzles with a twist. You can check them out at our website.

Via our website you can also order plays in a format that is ideally suited for fund raising purposes, or just to engender community. With the scripts for each play we provide full formats of the evening suggestions, a quiz, in fact all that is required to put on a memorable evening of entertainment with little effort.

For further details, and to purchase any of our publications, please go to: http://galacticpublishers.net/

We look forward to meeting your ongoing reading pleasure needs.

Galactic Publishers Limited